EMBRACING *Your* POWER

A Woman's Path to Authentic Leadership
& Meaningful Relationships

EMBRACING

Your

POWER

MARSHA L. CLARK

GREENLEAF
BOOK GROUP PRESS

Published by Greenleaf Book Group Press
Austin, Texas
www.gbgpress.com

Distributed by Greenleaf Book Group

For ordering information or special discounts for bulk purchases, please contact Greenleaf Book Group at PO Box 91869, Austin, TX 78709, 512.891.6100.

Design and composition by Greenleaf Book Group and Teresa Muñiz
Cover design by Greenleaf Book Group and Teresa Muñiz
"Embrace Your Greatness" by Lynette Ann Lane. Copyright © by Lynette Ann Lane.

For permission to reproduce copyrighted material, grateful acknowledgment is made to the following sources:
Chart "Sleep Duration Recommendations." Copyright © by the National Sleep Foundation. Reproduced by permission of the National Sleep Foundation.
"Our Deepest Fear" from *A Return to Love: Reflections on the Principles of "A Course in Miracles."* Copyright © by Marianne Williams. Reproduced by permission of HarperPerennial, a division of HarperCollins.
"Nine Steps to Forgiveness" by Fred Luskin. From *Greater Good Magazine.* September 1, 2004. Copyright © 2004 by Fred Luskin. Reproduced by permission of the author. https://greatergood.berkeley.edu/article/item/nine_steps_to_forgiveness
From "Male and Female Brains: Are They Wired Differently?" by Dr. Rob Pascale and Dr. Louis Primavera, from *Psychology Today,* April 25, 2019. https://www.psychologytoday.com/us/blog/so-happy-together/201904/male-and-female-brains. Copyright © 2019 by Dr. Rob Pascale and Dr. Louis Primavera. Reproduced by permission of the authors and *Psychology Today.*

Credits continued on page 317, which serves as an extension of the copyright page.

Publisher's Cataloging-in-Publication data is available.

Print ISBN: 978-1-62634-895-0

eBook ISBN: 978-1-62634-896-7

Part of the Tree Neutral® program, which offsets the number of trees consumed in the production and printing of this book by taking proactive steps, such as planting trees in direct proportion to the number of trees used: www.treeneutral.com

TreeNeutral®

Printed in the United States of America on acid-free paper

21 22 23 24 25 26 27   10 9 8 7 6 5 4 3 2 1

First Edition

This book is dedicated to my grandchildren, Georgia, Jackson, and Margaret. May they live in a world where women and girls are valued and treated equally.

CONTENTS

ACKNOWLEDGMENTS

When I was in the process of developing the Power of Self Program more than twenty years ago, I sought and received plenty of feedback. To my knowledge, there was nothing in the market similar to what I was designing. I passionately shared my vision of what elements the program would be comprised of and the benefits it would offer to participants, their organizations, their clients, and society on a larger level. I would describe the responses as fitting into two distinct categories. The first category was avid support and a belief that I could make it happen. The second was more of "great idea, and good luck with that." The skepticism was palpable. Both were most helpful. The former gave me the courage and confidence to keep going. The latter prepared me for the naysayers, critics, and less-than-willing prospects that were an inevitable part of selling the program.

I would like to start by thanking my family. My husband Dale was an extraordinary supporter and teacher. He helped me to see things from a male point of view that was instructive rather than superior. He spent many head and heart hours encouraging me, helping me find my courage when things were scary, and keeping me balanced when I found myself on the extreme edges. My son Brent was part of the Clark team. He offered a perspective that reflected a younger generation. He eventually even participated in forums where he described the experience and the value of being a supportive and strong man by acknowledging and valuing the contributions of women on all fronts. Brent married his wonderful and powerful wife, Claire, and they are now parents to my three amazing grandchildren: Georgia, Jackson, and

Margaret. Admittedly, they are my extra special "lab experience." I see them playing out some stereotypes and contradicting others. They make me proud and give me hope for a future world that values women and girls as amazing and valuable contributors the world over.

My extended family also includes Natalie Hollingsworth and Misty Moore. They are my left and right hands. I could not do what I do without them. They organize my life, support all aspects of the business, and are truly good people who live the values and principles described in this book. A special thanks to Clete Smith for his encouragement and unwavering support.

The people who helped design and develop the program that led to this book are: Denice Autry, Nadine Bell, Janice Burres, Brent Clark, Jennifer Cobo Cannon, Michelle Davidson, Ann Cohen, Mary Dean, Nancy Long, Ann Lau, LeeAnn Mallory, Renee Moorefield, Phil Novick, Kathy Palmer, Denise Renter, Lynne Sheppard, Tracie Shipman, and Lynn Womble. This team was instrumental in making sure we covered the right topics in a way that resonated with women. They did curriculum reviews to find or create the best content. They helped design the interactive exercises and the helpful tools. They were a great team to work with and made sure we got the job done—the job of creating a superior quality learning experience.

My associates—both coaches and facilitators—reflect the very best. They are pioneers in their own rights and ensured we kept the principles of the Power of Self current and rich. They are: Michelle Adams, Rita Andrews, Eddie Batten, Patricia Berger, Jane Cocking, La Rue Eppler, Dottie Gandy, Denise Kirkman, Judith Leibowitz, Anne Litwin, Peg Long, Lee Ann Mallory, Amber Mayes, Mary Lou Michael, Renee Moorefield, Patricia Parham, Cindy Pladziewicz, Valerie Prater, Denise Renter, Lorna Rickard, Tracie Shipman, Amy Rojas, Susie Vaughan, Suzanne Zaldivar, Suzanne Zeman, and Meridan Zerner.

I also want to thank the many great leaders I worked for at Electronic Data Systems (EDS): Jeff Heller, Dean Linderman, Jim Meler, Gary

Rudin, and Stuart Reeves, in particular. You taught me so much and believed in me when I didn't believe in myself. And you afforded me opportunities to lead in ways I could never have imagined. I would be remiss if I didn't thank Peter Koestenbaum. Though he wasn't an EDS employee, he was an amazing mentor to me while I was there. He deepened my knowledge and my skills regarding leadership. I also want to call out the great team I had in my first account executive role. I called this time a leader's Camelot experience—all things were so good! My time at EDS shaped my leadership beliefs and principles, and those have served me well in my lifetime.

I would also like to acknowledge the small and mighty team that helped make this book a reality: Natalie Hollingsworth, Misty Moore, Helen Chang, Wendi McGowan-Ellis, and Tracie Shipman. The staff at Greenleaf Book Group were invaluable in helping me convey my story and my messages in a most useful and meaningful way: Sally Garland, Ava Coibion, Elizabeth Brown, Pam Nordberg, Teresa Muñiz, Tyler LeBleu, Corrin Foster, and Kristine Peyre-Ferry.

INTRODUCTION

This book has been a long time in the making. Over twenty years ago, I had a vision of helping women achieve success based on *their* definition of success rather than what someone else wanted for them or from them. To this day, my wish is for them to hold on to themselves in the process, staying true to who they are rather than adopting a male model or profile of leadership.

Every person has both masculine and feminine traits, characteristics, and strengths. What is key is that women avoid placing restrictions on their paths to success based on how we have traditionally defined those inherent qualities. Beware of self-created obstacles! Each one of us is ultimately a complex individual capable of growing our strengths and diminishing our weaknesses. I want us to be able to tap into our authentic selves so we can be the best that we can be.

BACKGROUND

This may sound strange to some and familiar to others. I grew up in an era where women were told we could be whatever we wanted to be, but the reality was that women were either nurses, schoolteachers, secretaries, or stay-at-home moms . . . all wonderful and respected professions and choices. But where were the opportunities and examples to be astronauts, engineers, lawyers, doctors, and business executives?

I started my "corporate" career as a typist working in the typing pool of a federal government agency. I loved business and commerce and was eager to learn more about leadership, customers, and employees.

I finished that career as an officer of a publicly traded Fortune 50 company twenty-seven years later. I learned so much in those twenty-seven years, from both good and bad bosses, peers, direct reports, and the customers themselves. What I knew when I left the corporate world was that I wanted to support women in meaningful ways, and I believed that leadership was the key ingredient.

People often ask, "Why a leadership program specifically for women?" Here is what I would offer, based on over twenty years of experience:

- Women tend to ask more questions—more specifically, their *real* questions—and, therefore, engage and learn more when there are only women in the group. They ask questions they wouldn't ask if men were in the room. This isn't about male bashing; this is about empathy and acceptance.

- Women frequently feel isolated in their organizations, often finding themselves as the only or one of few women in the room. Having a chance to talk with and create support among other women who have similar challenges, issues, and opportunities helps them realize they are not alone and that nothing is wrong with them. It gives them greater confidence in successfully addressing their own challenges, issues, and opportunities.

- Networking in a developmental setting leads to building trust and support for one another, optimizing individual and organizational performance. It can also lead to new business opportunities.

- Gender differences can subtly impact a woman's ability to move up in an organization. Professional women differ from men in style, not in skill. We teach to those differences and play to a woman's inherent (and certainly developable!) strengths.

- Women often don't have clarity about what they want for themselves and, therefore, don't always ask for what they want. Programs emphasizing self-awareness, deeper understanding, clarifying choices, taking action, and reflecting on outcomes can generate enormous improvements in effectiveness and achieving desired results when it comes to charting a trajectory for a woman's future.

So, I pondered my own options and I became an entrepreneur—not by some grand design or burning passion but rather because I wanted to do it my way. My way was through *collaboration* and partnering rather than only *competing*, by really developing provocative and significant learning experiences.

For the next fifteen months, I organized a group of women and a few dear and enlightened men, and we met one weekend a month to discuss the possibilities available in forming an organization designed to empower women in the workplace. We invited many different points of view on what a great leadership program for women would include. Through exploring the competitive marketplace, we determined who our competitors might be. We attended workshops and programs that we thought reflected content we wanted to include in our program. We pushed our ideas and created new possibilities from our collaborative approach. Engineers, doctors, lawyers, analysts, consultants, instructional designers, and a wide variety of business and organizational leaders came together to create this great program, along with other learning opportunities. We also conducted focus groups, which enabled us to gather information from potential participants, diversity professionals, human resources leaders, and businesspeople (because they were the people who would eventually write the checks). I used every business skill I had ever learned, along with my networking and relationship skills, to make it happen.

I felt as if everything I had done to this point had prepared me for what was to come.

After months of research, design, and development, the Power of Self Program was launched in September 2001. That, of course, is a memorable month and year in America, when we experienced the 9/11 terrorist attacks that would rearrange the world as we knew it. The country, and I, was reeling. We had women registered for the program and ready to go, and then everything fell into uncertainty. To make a long story short, I crunched numbers, had long discussions with my husband Dale, and we decided to give the program away the first year. It was a $350,000 decision, which was huge for us.

Many trusted, well-intentioned male colleagues offered the conventional wisdom that if participants didn't pay for it, they wouldn't value it. That didn't sound right to me, and I can tell you that my instincts were right. Over the last twenty years, I've enjoyed valuable business partnerships from many of the women in that inaugural program. I can't begin to predict what would have happened had we waited.

What I know is that we were poised and ready, and I didn't want to lose momentum. No matter what happened in our country, we needed great leadership, and if we needed to flex with potential subsequent events, we would. And so, twenty-six women embarked on a learning journey spanning twenty-three days, delivered in seven sessions over nine months. We haven't looked back since.

When we conducted our competitive analysis in 2000, there was only one other commercial women's leadership program that we would consider true competition. It was called "The Bully School" and came complete with a tagline: "Where women come to smooth off their rough edges."

Well, that was quite representative of the thinking at that time. Since that inaugural launch, hundreds of women have gone through the Power of Self Program and the many programs it has spawned—both in-house programs as well as other public programs. Women from more than sixty countries have attended our programs over the past twenty years. I hope this book will extend our reach even further.

Let me be clear—we never set out to "fix" women. We're perfectly fine just the way we are. We did want our program to help women discover and rediscover themselves by developing our authentic leadership strengths and styles. This isn't about conforming to someone else's definition of leadership or success. *It's all about you and what you want*—and not in a selfish or self-serving way. Rather, the goal is to put yourself back on your own to-do list, while replenishing yourself, so that you can be more resourceful.

Women do so many things for everyone else, and we often forget to take care of ourselves. But we can do things for others—many wonderful and giving things—while also putting our visions, goals, and needs in the forefront of our imagination and focus. Isn't that refreshing!

As I prepared to write this book, I have been challenged by how to capture all of the nuggets and nuances without overwhelming my readers. (Think of that huge stack of books on your bedside table.) I started out thinking that the content I wished to include would amount to one book but quickly realized that I could easily fill eight hundred pages. I felt that the sheer volume of the book would not make it an inviting read. With much agonizing over several months, I have decided to write three books that cover five different topics under the heading of the Power of Self Leadership Series:

- *Embracing Your Power: A Woman's Path to Authentic Leadership and Meaningful Relationships*

- *Expanding Your Power: A Woman's Opportunity to Inspire Teams and Influence Organizations*

- *Enriching Your Power: A Woman's Choice to Lift Others Up*

Though the first book, *Embracing Your Power*, takes us through parts 1 and 2, an overview of parts 3 through 5 will be beneficial so you can have a preview of the overall trajectory of the program. I believe this structure will provide the most effective way to learn and apply what you're learning. Before we get started on hardcore content, let me share two things with you that are critical to the program: 1) Design Principles and 2) Foundational Elements.

DESIGN PRINCIPLES

Design Principles are something like a road map. They provide a big-picture view of the path to get you to your destination. This big-picture view did not immediately come to me or to those who helped in assembling this program overnight, and we had to do substantial "homework" in the creation of our blueprint. We relied on an array of diversity professionals, leadership development professionals, and business professionals for evaluation. The goal: a program that would endure the test of time and feel trustworthy to its valuable clients. For this reason, our nontraditional method had to possess strong bones . . . or Design Principles. The Power of Self Program and this book are designed in the following way:

Part 1:

Focuses on **self-awareness** or **self-knowledge**. I often describe this learning journey as an inside-out approach. It starts with me. What are my strengths? What are my patterns of behavior? What are my automatic or default behaviors? Do others see me as I see myself?

Conventional leadership wisdom says that one of the biggest derailers or show-stoppers for leadership effectiveness is a lack of self-awareness. I think I'm showing up to the world one way, and the world is seeing me quite differently. This gap can get me in trouble if I don't understand my blind spots. In this first section of the book, we'll focus on who you are as a woman and how we often differ from men, who you are as a woman leader, and who you are as a *powerful* woman leader, prioritizing leading from your strengths and values in a most authentic way.

Part 2:

Focuses on our **interpersonal relationships**, specifically with other women. One of the values prioritized in my work is about women supporting women—I cannot stress enough the importance of this goal.

This shift in how women interact within their professional relationships has come a long way and is one of the biggest changes I've seen since starting this work twenty years ago. Back then, women were competitive with (often with a smile on our faces) and critical of other women. The way I understand this is that many women had fought so hard for a seat at the table—and those seats were precious and rare—that we didn't initially consider the importance of opening up or adding more chairs for other women. Women now understand the importance and power of supporting other women. This concept became so clear when I read the book by Gail Evans, *She Wins, You Win: The Most Important Rule Every Businesswoman Needs to Know*. Published in 2003, Ms. Evans's book still has great relevance today.

We'll explore how women can be misogynistic to other women. We'll discuss why you can't put all women in the same bucket—that women are diverse across many categories. Bottom line, how do we embrace our own woman-ness and that of other women as well?

Part 2 also focuses on interpersonal relations across both genders. Research shows that building trust is foundational to all relationships, and we all know that well-formed, healthy relationships are crucial to leadership, customers, and business results. We'll share a trust model, a betrayal continuum, and how to heal from betrayal. We'll also spend considerable time on setting and maintaining boundaries; letting others enter our safe space is one of the ways we betray ourselves. We'll also spend time talking about managing conflict and enriching relationships.

There is much written about women's response to discord—namely, we tend to avoid conflict and often accommodate others during conflict situations. We'll give you more tools in your tool kit for managing conflict and enriching relationships.

The first two parts are what I refer to as "embracing your power." We'll then expand and enrich your power in the Power of Self Leadership Series.

Part 3:

Focuses on **team or group dynamics**. The information and tools shared are applicable whether you are a team leader, supervisor, manager, director, or even operating at an executive level. As you think about your own career aspirations, leading a team may be part of that aspiration. This information and these tools will help you make the transition from individual contributor to leader of a team.

We explore our female needs around inclusion, control, and openness; developing a new team; creating a high-performance team culture; and making decisions. This part includes ample tools, frameworks, and even language to gain clarity about your intentions and how to execute your plan.

Part 4:

Focuses on the **organizational aspect of leadership**. We'll help you better understand organization dynamics. Organizations are complex. There are plans, policies, processes, and people involved.

We'll look at how organizations work through the lens of four roles that are present regardless of what kind of organization you're in. The four roles are Tops, Middles, Bottoms, and Customers. We can play any one of those roles on any given day. For example, if you're meeting with your direct reports, you're a Top. If you're meeting with your boss, you're a Bottom. If your boss, your team, and you are meeting, you're a Middle. If you are on the receiving end of a product or service—whether internal or external to your organization—you're a Customer.

We'll explore how each of those roles has some unique characteristics and challenges and how we can develop effective strategies for effective leadership regardless of role and regardless of gender.

We'll also share information on how to have courageous group conversations, including a process to teach you how to work with your team to "name elephants" or discuss the undiscussables. And to wrap it up, we'll share information and tools to help women ask for what they want, influence outcomes, and prepare for negotiations.

Part 5:

Focuses on **women in the world**, and I know that sounds pretty lofty. We'll share information on social norms from country to country, as well as information on the condition or status of women around the world. I often think of this content as broadening our perspective beyond our titles, organizations, industries, and nations.

We then focus on managing our careers with intentionality. What are the myths? What is the definition of the "ideal worker"? How do you define a high-potential employee? How do I figure out what I really want to do? My experience in working with both men and women is that men are often clearer and more specific in their career goals compared to women, who are more vague or uncertain.

Finally, we'll wrap it all up, encouraging you to create your own leadership stand—defining who you are as a leader. What are your leadership principles, values, philosophies? We'll encourage you to share these ideas with those around you—your family, boss, peers, team members, customers. You can think of the definition of who you are as a leader as your brand. Of course, it's a dynamic document. As we learn, evolve, and mature, we're always refining and getting clearer.

Hopefully, this design helps you see the big picture, how it all fits together. I encourage you to read and study one part, then go and apply what you've learned. There is evidence that the learn-practice-learn-practice approach ensures that the learning is applied and is more sustainable.

FOUNDATIONAL ELEMENTS

I want to share what I call the Foundational Elements. I often refer to them as the threads that run throughout the various parts of this book. We'll refer to them often as we move through the content.

ELEMENT 1:
Building Your Tool Kit

Knowing which tool to use when is what differentiates great leaders from good leaders. Good leaders know they have a tool kit and are always trying to enrich that tool kit. Great leaders know which tool to use when. The more tools I have, the more options I have. Knowing which tool to use, and when, is a differentiator for great and effective leadership. This book is full of tools. I think of tools as models, frameworks, checklists, relevant questions, quotes, and values.

ELEMENT 2:
Understanding the Answer to Every Leadership
Question Is . . . "It Depends"

I want to reinforce that there is rarely one way to do most things. If there were one leadership answer to most questions, we would all have that book in our libraries, and it would be worn and tattered from constant use. We have to understand our objectives, who we're working with, how to balance results with relationships, and so many other variables.

ELEMENT 3:
Aligning Clarity, Courage, and Timing

- **Clarity** – The best leaders have to get clear on their objectives and their intentions, as well as how they want to show up from a leadership perspective. If we aren't clear to begin with, we often end up in a place we don't want to be.

- **Courage** – I like to refer to a Winston Churchill quote on this topic: "It takes courage to know when to stand up and speak, and it takes courage to know when to sit down and listen." His statement is a variation on knowing which tool to use when.

- **Timing** – This is often tricky. Questions surrounding timing can include the following: Do I need to do the "meetings before the meetings" to vet this proposal or recommendation? (The answer is almost always yes, especially on the big-ticket items.) Do I bring it up in the meeting if I feel strongly about it? If so, how can I best be heard? What follow-up meetings do I need to have to ensure we drive to results?

My wish is that you have greater skills in doing your job, executing your plans, and achieving desired results after reading this book. Thinking these pieces through as a part of our planning process, as well as scheduling the actual meetings, needs to happen on the front end. It brings us right back to clarity.

ELEMENT 4:
Slowing Down to Speed Up

This element may be my favorite. Women (as well as men) are running, running, running all day long. I often think about it as jumping from one gerbil wheel to the next gerbil wheel. We go on automatic pilot and try to get it all done, checked off the to-do list. Because we're always running, we don't always do our best work. We have long prided ourselves on being awesome multitasking women. Now there are articles telling us all the multitasking may be leading to adult attention deficit disorder. We seem to sometimes be more focused on getting everything done rather than working on the most important tasks that are truly going to make a difference. If we don't slow down, how do we get clear? If we're not clear, how do we know what to work on? We can take a few precious moments on a Friday and check our calendar to ensure that our schedule for the following week truly reflects the highest priority work. We'll talk more about this when we talk about setting priorities, managing our time, and delegating in chapter 6. Slow down. Take a breath. You've earned it.

ELEMENT 5:
Asking Myself, "What Else Could Be True?"

This question has helped me so many times. As human beings, we are good at making up stories. And in those stories, we are often the *victim* ("Poor, pitiful me") or the *know-it-all* ("I told you it wouldn't work, and now look where we are") or the *heroine* (riding in to save the day). None of those stories serves us particularly well.

The teaching point here is not on whether we should or shouldn't make up a story. We will. It's human nature. Rather, our choice point comes from whether we're going to hold on to that story and convince ourselves it's true.

So, here's what I do that helps me to let go of that story or, at least, hold it lightly. When I hear someone say something that I consider wrong, or someone who is being critical, or someone who is judging or blaming another person, I say to myself, *Isn't that fascinating!* And then I ask myself, *What else could be true?* The "fascinating" reminder takes me from a place of judging, criticizing, and blaming to a place of curiosity. Thus, in thinking, "What else could be true?" I remind myself that I made up the first story, so I'm certainly capable of making up a different story, perhaps one that is more productive to achieving our desired outcomes. Better yet, if I get curious, I can ask questions and learn more to get the real story. This process requires practice and slowing down. As I said, this practice has helped me so much to stay engaged in the conversation, drive for results, and build more meaningful relationships.

ELEMENT 6:
Creating a Plan

In absence of a leader, be one. I don't mean only when the leader is physically absent. I'm talking about when leaders get stuck and don't know what to do next. When things are overwhelming to some people, they shut down. Others may throw some spaghetti at the wall and see what sticks. And others may find great help in *collaborating*. Shutting down is the least acceptable option. Make all mistakes at full speed and don't make the same one twice.

I learned this from one of my favorite leaders. I had achieved my first more senior-level position and was one of the first women to get there. I was nervous and hoped I was up for the job. And then, my boss was sent on a temporary assignment that was all encompassing. I talked to him for about thirty minutes a month. He had more faith in me than I had in myself. He gave me the preceding advice and he "protected" me if I screwed up too badly. It was one of the most significant learning experiences of my career.

ELEMENT 7:
Learning Agility

As a lifelong learner and one who has *Learner* in her Top 5 strengths in her StrengthsFinder evaluation, this one is near and dear to my heart. I started out my corporate career in a typing pool and ended up as a corporate officer. Learning agility played a major role in making that happen.

There are three learning agility questions that I ask often:

- What did I do?

- What did I learn?

- How will this help me going forward?

Sometimes, I ask these questions on a daily basis, but more typically on a weekly basis. These moments of reflection allow me to make sure that I don't "make the same mistake twice." Asking the questions also allows me to be more effective the next time around because I slowed down to get clear about what worked and what didn't work. When I coach and mentor people, I ask these questions early and often. As a leader, it's my job to develop others and help them learn critical thinking skills. These three questions go a long way in helping me do that.

ELEMENT 8:
Creating Capacity in Others

A primary responsibility of every leader is to help others learn, grow, and achieve their career aspirations. As women, we're often accustomed to taking care of, or coordinating, all activities pertaining to our results. Research has shown that women tend to be perfectionists more than men.

Ladies, we're going to have to let that go. How can we learn to delegate and hold other people accountable? How can we let someone do it their way and be okay with that? For example, how can we learn to not take over someone else's incomplete assignment and finish the rest of the work ourselves, simply because we can "do it in less time"? These questions will be explored throughout this book. There is the principle of "what got you here won't get you there." We have to let go and share knowledge with, develop skills in, and provide coaching and feedback to others so they can continue to grow and take on more responsibilities.

If it took me over sixty years to become who I am today, I'm not going to flip a switch or read a book and change overnight, and I certainly don't expect that from you. The goal is truly about learning and practicing over and over again as our lives continue to evolve in an ever-changing world.

I hope that by reading these foundational elements you're more excited than ever to continue reading this book. I know time is limited for us all, and most of us typically have several books stacked on our bedside table or queued up on our electronic devices. Take this book a chapter at a time. Soak it in. Practice or apply what you've learned. Share and discuss it with others.

Now, let's get started! Join me as I take you on a learning journey with real tools and stories to help you be the best leader you can be—personally and professionally.

PART 1

EXPLORING POWER

CHAPTER 1

WHAT IS POWER?

A woman who is in full possession of her mind,
who is responsible for her thoughts and actions,
and who is unafraid of bucking the status quo is a
dangerous woman. Such a woman is a force of nature.
She creates whirlwinds of change in individuals,
communities, and systems just by being herself.

~ Dawn Marie Daniels and Candace Sandy,
Souls of My Sisters

This chapter is about exploring who we are as women, as woman leaders, and as *powerful* woman leaders. Each of us is a unique combination of biology, genetics, life experiences, and social conditioning. Over time, we develop habits and defaults, along with patterns of thinking, talking, and behaving. We often operate on autopilot, not even thinking about what just happened or what happens next. Let's take a moment to discover the origins of some of those automatic tendencies and examine our choices moving forward.

I like to move directly into an exercise. Let's explore how we define what it means to be powerful.

POWERFUL WOMEN ARE . . .

ACTIVITY:

Complete these sentences. Repeat each sentence stem three times. Don't over-think it. Don't fret about being politically correct. Write down the first thing that comes to your mind. There are no right or wrong answers.

Powerful women are

_____

Powerful women are

_____

Powerful women are

_____

Powerful men are

- -

Powerful men are

- -

Powerful men are

- -

Powerless women are

_____

Powerless women are

_____

Powerless women are

_____

Powerless men are

- -

Powerless men are

- -

Powerless men are

- -

REFLECTIONS:

What do you notice about your answers? Are the answers for powerful or powerless women and men similar or different? If different, in what ways? How would you interpret those differences? And where do they come from? What beliefs do you hold that prompt these responses?

Did someone's face pop into your head based on any one of the four sentence stems? If yes, did you then think of words or phrases that described that person?

Where do you see yourself in your responses? Do you strive to be powerful? How might that aspirational list describing powerful women be daunting? Inspiring?

Were you surprised by any of your responses? If so, in what way?

How might these beliefs impact your relationships with other women? Other men?

How do you feel about the concept of power? I have found it to be an uncomfortable word for women. However, we regularly face this reality in our lives. We might think about people who have had power over us in a negative or limiting way, or even an abusive way. I have found myself behaving as both a powerful and a powerless woman, and I've heard many women say the same thing. Power is tricky, and there are many lenses through which to view it. I offer three ways to think about power—all of which are valid and appropriate when used intentionally and effectively.

- **Positional Power**: This kind of power, hierarchical in nature, refers to a level or title in an organizational or institutional structure. For example, a vice president typically has more positional power or authority than a senior manager. Someone else bestows or gives you positional power. They hire you into the organization with a certain title or promote you to a new role with a specific title. Now, consider this: if someone gives you positional or hierarchical power, they can also take it away. I refer to this as "outside-in" power. Women often think about this as "power over others," which often conjures up a negative connotation. It may even be hard for us to assert our positional power, and yet that is often a requirement of organizational leadership.

- **Relational Power**: This kind of power requires at least two people. You and I choose to engage as partners or as part of a larger team to do something that neither of us could do on our own. Thus, we have relational power or a greater collective power. We make individual choices of when to and when not to engage in such a relationship.

- **Personal Power**: I have personal power when I am making my own intentional choices. No other human bestows personal power on me. My choices are whether to hold on to this personal power, share this power, or give away this power. An example of holding on to this power is when I have clarity and speak my point of view in discussions or meetings, acting with integrity and respect for myself and others. Conversely, giving away my personal power occurs when I don't set or maintain healthy boundaries, say "yes" when I want to say "no," don't ask for what I need, or work unhealthy hours to achieve a desired outcome. I refer to this as "inside-out" power. Personal power is my favorite because it is always available to me and doesn't depend on someone else's actions. I display my personal power no matter what role I have in any given scenario, whether it be personal or professional.

ACTIVITY 1:

Think about a recent situation in which you've held on to your personal power.

What led to the behaviors and actions that resulted in you holding on to your personal power?

How can you be more conscious and intentional to repeat this behavior or this approach?

ACTIVITY 2:

Think about a recent situation in which you've given your personal power away.

What led to your behaviors and actions that prompted you to give your power away?

Are there patterns you can identify that often lead to you giving your power away (e.g., certain people, certain circumstances, certain beliefs)?

POWER SOURCES

Let's dig a little deeper into this concept of power.

ACTIVITY:

Think about a time when you felt powerful. Capture a few notes describing that time. (And for you mothers out there, I encourage you to think about a time other than when you were giving birth. We'll give you that one!)

Where were you? Was anyone there with you?

What were you feeling emotionally? Physically?

What would you consider your sources of power to be? In other words, what helped you to experience this powerful moment? Write down as many things as possible.

Thoughts to consider:

- Sometimes it is hard for women to recall powerful moments. We often don't think in those terms. I invite you to notice when you're feeling powerful and reflect on how you got there.

- As I mentioned earlier, I have often found myself feeling powerless. I go quiet. I don't ask for what I need. I let someone else have way too much impact on my mood for the day. When I find myself in one of those powerless moments, my choice point is not whether I'm going to feel powerless—I already do. My choice point is whether I'm going to stay in that powerless place, wallowing in the powerlessness. When you find yourself feeling powerless, pull out your list of power sources, be they family members or friends, or your own life experience. Your power may be found in your faith or in tangible abstracts such as coaching, preparation, knowledge, determination, willpower, or clarity. Better yet, do this activity with other women and compare notes. Add to your list of power sources. You have more available to you than you have yet realized or used.

CHAPTER 2

A LESSON IN CONTRASTS

The most common way we give up power
is by thinking we don't have any.

~ Alice Walker

The emphasis in this chapter is on some of the subtle, subconscious, or unconscious ways that men and women show up differently. Many studies over the years have demonstrated that a woman can do something almost identically as a man, yet it will be interpreted quite differently. For the women who have been pioneers in their organizations by assuming leadership roles, we recognized it was a tricky playing field. If we acted "too much like a man" we were often labeled negatively. If we acted "too much like a woman" we were often labeled as "too soft and fuzzy" or "too touchy-feely" or "too emotional." It was a fine line to navigate.

A woman once told me that she had a strange experience over a several-year time span. She couldn't walk past a Victoria's Secret store without going in and buying some sort of feminine lingerie. She had never done this before. She had grown up in an era where women's suits were similar to men's, swapping out a skirt for women rather than men's trousers. She finally came to realize that she was trying to hold on to her feminine self by wearing feminine lingerie under that male-fashioned suit.

When she shared her story, women were ready to share their versions of these kinds of stories. Dress codes may have changed over the years, but women are still struggling with how to fit in. Remember the cigar-smoking phase? Or asking yourself if you should learn to play golf? Or avoiding the Monday morning coffee discussions about the weekend's big sporting event? Or declining (and maybe you weren't even invited) to the executive retreat at your fellow executive's hunting cabin? The list goes on and on. Even if you have landed an office in the executive suite, these questions and this sort of exclusion still occur today. I hear some version of it in all of my programs and over half of my coaching conversations.

So where does all this come from? Is it nature or nurture? The answer to this last question is "yes." We all maintain stereotypes and unconscious biases that are automatic, unintentional, deeply ingrained, universal, and able (and likely) to influence our behavior. In this chapter, we're going to explore stereotypes, invisible differences, male and female brains, and something called the "impostor syndrome."

As you read this chapter, keep in mind these two factors: 1) The research included here is based on a bell-shaped curve. There are always exceptions on either end of that curve. And as much as we want to believe these things no longer happen, I want to ensure you they do. I hear about them routinely in programs where women often talk about experiences they've otherwise never shared, and in coaching calls where women are asking for help on how to address these challenges.

And 2) Research continues to be done, and we continue to learn. Because an increasing number of women are entering senior roles, we have more data for our studies. My belief is that, as more women move into these influential roles, we can "change the system" by challenging the status quo, bringing a new and different perspective to the table, and offering different solutions for existing issues. I encourage each of you to continue to observe, notice, read about, and reflect on what you see and experience as you navigate an ever-changing landscape.

STEREOTYPES

Stereotypes are everywhere, and we all hold them. The official definition of gender stereotypes is: "expectations of behavior based on gender." In other words, when we walk into the room as women, others believe that we should behave a certain way simply because we are women.

Gender schema theory was introduced by psychologist Sandra Bem and asserted that children learn about male and female roles from the culture in which they live. According to the theory, children adjust their behavior to align with the gender norms of their culture from the earliest stages of social development. Gender schemas have an impact not only on how people process information, but also on the attitudes and beliefs that direct "gender-appropriate behavior."

There are many levels of stereotypes: geographical, generational, religious, and gender—just to name a few. We're going to explore gender biases about women. Let's start by pondering a few questions.

REFLECTIONS:

How does your life differ from that of your mother's or grandmother's? What stereotypes existed for them? How are they different for you?

What messages did you receive early on in your life about what it meant to be a "good girl"? How have those played out in your adult life?

What stereotypes do you hold about women from different generations?

What stereotypes do you hold about women from different geographies?

What stereotypes do you hold about gender roles? (For instance: Women do housework, and men do yardwork.)

How can you raise your awareness, your consciousness about the stereotypes you hold?

What gender stereotyping messages are you sending, intentionally or unintentionally, to the young girls in your life?

How can you be more intentional about getting past your stereotypes to see the person rather than the stereotypes?

If either gender behaves outside of their culture's gender stereotype norms, they are often subjected to societal disapproval. People—both men and women—will often feel pressured to alter their behavior, or face rejection by those who disapprove of them.

ATTRIBUTE CHECKLIST

Based on Dr. Bem's work, I created an assessment that might help you to further explore your own attitudes and behaviors regarding certain attributes.

The instructions for completing the checklist are pretty simple. You will rate each attribute as high, medium, or low. If you feel strongly that you frequently display that At Work, score it "high." If you feel that you do not display that attribute very often, or display minimal traces of it, score it "low." If you are in the middle, score it "medium." There are two columns for each attribute: "At Work" and "Not at Work." Do not leave any blank spaces. Then score yourself on the second form.

Checklist Activity: Rate yourself high, medium, or low for each attribute in each column.

Attribute	At Work	Not at Work
Acts as a Leader		
Affectionate		
Aggressive		
Ambitious		
Analytical		
Assertive		
Athletic		
Cheerful		
Childlike		
Compassionate		
Competitive		
Defends One's Belief		
Does Not Use Harsh Language		
Dominant		
Eager to Soothe Hurt Feelings		
Feminine		
Flatterable		
Forceful		
Gentle		
Gullible		

Attribute	At Work	Not at Work
Has Leadership Abilities		
Independent		
Individualistic		
Loves Children		
Loyal		
Makes Decisions Easily		
Masculine		
Self-Reliant		
Self-Sufficient		
Sensitive to the Needs of Others		
Shy		
Soft-Spoken		
Strong Personality		
Sympathetic		
Tender		
Understanding		
Warm		
Willing to Take a Stand		
Willing to Take Risks		
Yielding		

Based on the work of Dr. Sandra Bem.

ATTRIBUTE SCORING FORM

Masculine/Feminine Score Sheet

Score: Low = 1, Medium = 3, High = 5

Feminine	Score at Work	Score Not at Work	Masculine	Score At Work	Score Not at Work
Affectionate			Acts as a Leader		
Cheerful			Aggressive		
Childlike			Ambitious		
Compassionate			Analytical		
Does Not Use Harsh Language			Assertive		
Eager to Soothe Hurt Feelings			Athletic		
Feminine			Competitive		
Flatterable			Defends One's Beliefs		
Gentle			Dominant		
Gullible			Forceful		
Loves Children			Has Leadership Abilities		
Loyal			Independent		
Sensitive to the Needs of Others			Individualistic		
Shy			Makes Decisions Easily		
Soft-spoken			Masculine		
Sympathetic			Self-Reliant		
Tender			Self-Sufficient		
Understanding			Strong Personality		
Warm			Willing to Take a Stand		
Yielding			Willing to Take Risks		
TOTAL					

Source: Adapted by Marsha Clark & Associates from Sandra Bem

Author's Note: Some will read this list and say it is outdated or that this hasn't been their story or reality. Some will declare that some of the words are not gender specific. Congratulations to you if this isn't your experience, but it is the reality of many women the world over. Though the world is always changing, deeply held beliefs are hard to change. Will the "categorization" of these words change over time? I certainly hope so! This list certainly isn't etched in stone and will likely change, as will the world and the individuals inhabiting it. I invite you to take this information in, consider it, and observe male and female language and behavior regarding

these attributes. A woman in one of my classes experienced a strong reaction to the word "gullible"
as a feminine attribute. Before I could respond, another woman in the class, who has years of aca-
demic research experience, responded that many sales-training courses are built around a woman's
gullibility, especially in what are considered men's buying domains (cars, trucks, lawn equipment,
etc.). I offer this information and the exercise as a way of seeing ourselves through a different lens,
exploring our own stereotypes. I hope you'll see it as a tool to generate awareness, insights, under-
standing, and more effective behaviors.

INTERPRETING MY SCORES

First and foremost, there are no right and wrong scores. Each of us has
our own set of beliefs, experiences, and values, and has been socially
conditioned in a variety of ways. This is especially true if we are a group
of women from many parts of the world. No matter how people may
want to put all women into one neat category, each woman is different
from the next. And remember, each and every human being has both
masculine and feminine traits. As a result, feminine does not absolutely
equal female any more than masculine absolutely equals male. Each of
us, regardless of gender, can exhibit these attributes to varying degrees.

In reviewing your results, note where you score differently at work
versus not at work. How would you describe what is driving those differences? Are you strategically choosing to flex your behavior from one
environment to the other? Or are you trying to conform to someone
else's definition or stereotype of how you should act because you are a
woman? Whatever is driving your behavior matters. If you are being
strategic, it is empowering, because you choose to behave that way. It
is an example of you holding on to your power. It can give you energy.
On the other hand, if you are conforming to a certain stereotype to
please someone or fit in, it is disempowering and can be energy drain-
ing. One of the women in my early class described it like this: "Every
morning, just before the elevator doors open on my floor, I have to say
to myself, 'Showtime.'" She certainly wasn't happy as she was describing
the experience.

Admittedly, I made some assumptions early on that women would
generally have higher masculine scores in the "at work" boxes than they

would for the "not at work" ones. I have learned over the many years I've been using this assessment that many women have to "tone down" what they describe as their masculine tendencies at work because to act too far out of stereotype can cause them problems. They may be seen as too hard-hearted, aggressive, or ambitious. These behaviors can also get them labeled as various "B" words—bully, bitchy, bossy, bulldozer, or barracuda (to name a few that I've heard).

The important thing to remember is that all forty attributes are tools in your tool kit. And the best leaders know which tool to use when. There is a time for warmth and compassion, and a time for risk-taking and assertiveness. I am not suggesting that you be something you're not. My belief is that if you can be independent, self-sufficient, or any other traditionally masculine trait, then it *is* you.

Maybe you're willing to speak up and take a stand even though that is out of your comfort zone. Displaying such behaviors may not come as naturally, yet they are still available to you to use in certain situations. We need to get clear about which tool is the most effective to achieve the desired outcome. Then, we need to find the courage to use that tool, as well as plan and practice using the tool until we gain greater confidence and access to our enriched tool kit.

Last, we need to be aware of when we are applying stereotypes and when we are applying knowledge about a specific individual. We often focus on others applying stereotypes to us and how limiting that might be. We need to hold up the mirror to our own behaviors as well. Here are some things you might do to examine your own stereotypes and educate yourself along the way. Remember, as Maya Angelou said, "When we know better, we do better."

ACTIVITY:

Pick three to five characteristics about your background that you perceive as relatively unique in terms of your identity formation—as a woman or a woman of a certain race, age, religion, or national ethnicity. This could be about observed rituals, cultural practices, food, or certain stories or sayings passed down through your family. Explore the origins of these characteristics. When did you notice them? How have you practiced them? How might you be passing them along to your family?

Interview a person that you perceive as different from you. Ask them to share 3 to 5 characteristics that are unique and different about themselves based on their differences from you. This could be something to do with their age, gender, race, or any other category. Let them know that you are exploring your own stereotypes, and whatever questions you ask them you need to be prepared to answer about yourself. Ask them about the origin of their characteristics. Don't interrupt them, don't challenge them, and don't deny what they say. Take it in. Consider it. Respect their perspective. We cannot speak about the experience of another with any credibility.

Compare the things that make you and the other person similar yet different. Work hard to do this without applying judgmental thoughts or language (e.g., normal or not normal, better or worse, smart or not smart, etc.).

REFLECTIONS:

What stereotypes are you applying, consciously or unconsciously?

Think of how you would generally describe the following. Are your thoughts rooted in a stereotype? Are you applying one experience you've had to now describe a broader group?

- A woman who speaks up in a meeting
- A wealthy person
- A man who is ambitious, who everyone knows is climbing the ladder
- A woman who is ambitious, who everyone knows is climbing the ladder
- Working moms
- Stay-at-home moms
- People with tattoos or piercings
- Women wearing head coverings
- A small woman
- A large woman

Note: I didn't say this would be easy. Answer honestly.

Can you think of misperceptions you have had about people based on appearance, age, background, religion, ethnicity, political party affiliation, or socioeconomic status?

- How has this influenced or impacted your relationship with them?
- How have you been surprised after getting to know the person?
- How have your views changed after getting to know the person?

What stereotypes are you teaching or modeling for your children? Your colleagues? Others?

How will you catch yourself when you find yourself applying a stereotype? What will you do differently to get beyond the stereotype?

I will wrap up this discussion of stereotypes with this true story. A kindergarten teacher invited her students to come dressed as their favorite cartoon character. One little boy chose the character of Daphne from the cartoon *Scooby-Doo*. In other words, a five-year-old boy came dressed as a female cartoon character. How do you think his kindergarten classmates reacted? If you're like many with whom I've shared this story, you thought he was made fun of or bullied. The real result is that his classmates loved his costume. But the parents were a different story. They complained so loudly that the little boy was sent home confused and heartbroken. (And, by the way, my kindergarten teacher clients almost always get this answer right, as many of them have experienced variations of this story.)

The moral of this story is that we aren't born into this world with innate stereotypes, but we learn them through what we hear, see, and experience. My question for you is this—what are your words and actions saying about your stereotypes? What might you unknowingly be teaching others?

INVISIBLE DIFFERENCES

We frequently see women joining our programs who declare they aren't sure there are differences between men and women, especially as it relates to leadership. I don't know about you, but I believe that this 3 to 4 percent discrepancy matters. Keep in mind as you read this that each of us has both masculine and feminine characteristics in us. Masculine is not 100 percent male any more than feminine is 100 percent female.

Dr. Patricia Heim has spent over forty years studying gender differences. Her findings have resonated with hundreds of men and women around the world. As part of our research to find credible information that was relevant and insightful, Dr. Heim's work surged to the top of the list. I love her work because it isn't about good or bad, right or wrong—it is about being different. I love her point that if any of us were to go to a foreign country, we would expect the people there to speak a different language, to perhaps see things differently from us, and to display different behaviors or tendencies. As she describes it, men see themselves as being from their own country but women from a different country. They speak a different language and see things differently than many women do. And I want to remind you that the information I'm sharing with you is based on a bell-shaped curve. There are exceptions and outliers in every scenario.

THE FIRST 24 HOURS

Gender differences show up early. There is something referred to as the pink blanket–blue blanket studies. These studies have been done many times in many countries, and the results are consistent. The studies show that in the first twenty-four hours of a baby's life, boy babies notice noise, sound, and movement. Their eyes are drawn to the blinking lights on monitoring equipment in the hospital nursery, the movement of hospital staff as they cross the room, or any loud noises that might occur. Girls, on the flip side, look at their care-givers' faces—their eyes and mouths in particular—four hundred times more than boy babies. Yes, four hundred times more. I'll talk later about how these tendencies continue through childhood and even into adulthood.

One of the reasons I appreciate this research finding is related to the question about whether gender differences are innate or whether they are totally dependent on socialization. This evidence makes clear that certain gender differences are innate. Not a whole lot of social conditioning occurs in that first twenty-four hours.

CHILDHOOD LABELS

Another interesting finding relates to how childhood behaviors or tendencies play out differently from childhood to adulthood. If boys act too feminine, they are often called names. The acceptable range of gender-related behaviors for boys is much narrower than for girls. In the United States, if girls act masculine, they are called "tomboys." There are far fewer negative connotations for a girl being called a tomboy than, let's say, a boy being called a sissy or pansy.

As boys grow into men, if they display any feminine tendencies, they may be labeled a metrosexual or an enlightened male. Though such behavior may still prompt some harsh labeling, it is often seen as a strength, enabling greater versatility for relating to a broader range of people. As girls grow into women, if they continue to display masculine tendencies, they are harshly labeled an array of "B" words (remember bully, bossy, bitchy, barracuda, bulldozer).

Clearly, these labels are not synonymous with effective leadership when applied to women. I have laughingly said many times that I never knew that growing up a tomboy would be so helpful to me as an adult woman in business. Because I played with so many boys growing up, I learned how to survive and even thrive in a male-dominated environment. I also had greater practice developing my masculine attributes.

CHILDHOOD PLAY

Let's also discuss the research around the lessons of childhood play. As I see it, work is the adult version of play, and the rules we learn through our childhood games and activities are carried with us into our adult working lives.

Boys play games involving competition and a 50/50 chance of winning or losing. These childhood games teach boys to take a loss, drop it, and move on. Boys learn to relate to one another through conflict and are instructed by peers and adults that "it's not personal." They learn to do what the coach says and to play with other people they don't necessarily like. Boys learn not to cry and to mask their emotions in general, because when the game is over, it's over.

Girls play games that place value on getting along, being nice, and sharing equally, with little, if any, scorekeeping. When we're playing dolls or school or house, there is no scorekeeping and no explicit winners or losers. During some of my programs, I get pushback on this point based on the passage of Title IX of the Education Amendment Act of 1972 in the United States. This federal law opened up funding for sports for girls and certainly changed the playing field for actual scorekeeping games for girls.

Let me share a real-life story. Sara Tucholsky played softball for Western Oregon University. In the last college game Sara ever played, she came to bat in a 0–0 game against Central Washington that would decide which team would go to the NCAA Division II playoffs. The ball was pitched and Sara crushed it, sending it sailing over the fence for her first-ever home run. Sara hurt her knee as she rounded first base, and she went down. She later found out that she had torn the anterior cruciate ligament in her right knee. The rules of the game are that if one of her coaches or teammates had gone on the field to help her, she would have been called out. With Sara still lying in the dirt, the umpires and coaches quickly met. While the discussion was happening, the opposing team's first baseman Mallory Holtman asked a simple question, "Can I help her?" Mallory called on her shortstop Liz Wallace to help her. Together they asked Sara if they could pick her up. When Sara agreed, they hoisted her toward second base. Just as Sara was being lowered so she could touch second base, the cheering started and the video cameras fired up. People must have realized they were seeing the rarest of moments, competitors helping a fallen opponent, even when helping her would hurt their chances to win the game. When they lowered her to touch home, Sara said, "Thank you."

Fast-forward to the 2008 ESPY Awards, and there on stage were Sara, Mallory, and Liz accepting the "Best Moment" award. Yes, girls play competitive sports—and we do it our way.

Girls learn to personalize losses and avoid conflict because it hurts relationships. Girls learn to discuss things in hopes of avoiding conflicts or play only with those they consider "nice." Girls display emotions more easily because it's acceptable in their games, but they take disagreements as betrayals or being disloyal.

BEING AGGRESSIVE

Further related to these differences is how men and women being aggressive can be received and interpreted very differently. The Center for Creative Leadership has done multiple studies showing that both men and women need to be aggressive to be effective leaders. The differences are the range of acceptable emotions. Men have a much wider range of acceptable aggressive behavior. Relatively speaking, this range generally applies across industries and geographies. Women have a much narrower band of what's considered acceptable aggression, and it varies greatly across industries and geographies. For example, a woman has more latitude in manufacturing and construction industries than she does in education or nursing; likewise, she might find more room for aggression in New York than in Alabama, and more in the United States than in India or Dubai.

POWER AND LEADERSHIP STYLE

Now let's talk about differences in how men and women see power. Men are more prone to use hierarchical power. This relates to the positional power we talked about earlier. Most organizations—businesses, the military, government, and even religious organizations—are based on a hierarchical or masculine model of power. This is reflective of a one-up/one-down form of hierarchy. There is a pecking order: C-Suite, EVP, SVP, VP, etc., or head coach, star player, A-team, B-team, etc., or colonel, lt. colonel, major, captain, etc., or pope, cardinal, archbishop, bishop, priest, etc.

Men operate in this environment rather easily. They learn early on to run the play the coach calls because the coach has more positional power and authority. I once asked my husband Dale about what the point was of a drill sergeant saying, "Drop and give me forty!" His response (and he looked at me as if I had three heads) was, "I never bothered to ask."

The masculine model wasn't conceptually easy for me to understand, though I was expected to operate effectively in that environment. I also have to laugh every time a woman declares that she works in a male-dominated environment. I ask her to tell me one that is not. The common response is education and nursing. I then ask her if it is predominantly men or women on the boards, councils, or in the most senior positions in the education and health care worlds. The reality is, the people who make the decisions, have authority, and allocate resources will define the shape of their particular organization, industry, or institution. In almost all cases, that authority falls to men.

This hierarchical structure often lends itself to a command-and-control type of leadership, which can be very useful in crisis situations involving time-sensitive scenarios and safety considerations; it's also beneficial when there are no other options, because of governmental requirements, industry compliance, or in adherence to contract terms and conditions (e.g., the government says we have to do it, it's the law). Because many senior leaders and executives in the 1950s, 1960s, and even 1970s came from the military, this was a predominant style of leadership.

Women are often more comfortable in what Dr. Heim calls a flat structure or "power dead-even." In contrast to the one-up/one-down model, this is more of a model based on the notion that "we're all in this together." This is reflective of a more collaborative approach to leadership. Women like to ask for input, talk things over, and explore options. This approach is particularly effective when you are doing something brand new, you need multiple perspectives for a more comprehensive solution, you need their psychological buy-in, or you need a team to make it work.

I want to emphasize that a masculine versus feminine approach to leadership is not about right or wrong, good or bad. I take you back to the Foundational Elements: "Great leaders know what tool to use when." Every great leader has a rich tool kit and can flex her style or approach to achieve the desired outcome in service of the larger challenge or opportunity.

APPROACHING NEW SITUATIONS

When women approach new situations, they tend to tell you everything they don't know before they tell you what they do know. Dr. Heim describes it as "going into the confessional."

I can relate to this very well. I remember when I got the call from my boss telling me that, as of tomorrow, I was the president of the health care strategic business unit. It was a huge job and an important promotion. The first words out of my mouth were, "I don't know anything about health care. I'm so healthy and my family is, too. I haven't even filed a health claim in several years." My boss told me that he wasn't putting me there for my health care knowledge or experience. He was putting me there because of my leadership skills. I led a team of 2,500 competent health care technology professionals.

In her book about gender differences in work, author Sheryl Sandberg cites an example using a job posting with ten requirements. If a woman has eight of the ten requirements, she is likely to not apply. If a man has four of the ten requirements, he will apply. For the woman, it's a matter of fairness and honesty. "I want you to know what you're getting." For the man, it's a matter of adventure. "I'll tell them I can do it and then go figure out how." These are two very different ways of seeing, processing, and experiencing an opportunity.

LINGUISTIC PATTERNS

As we have all experienced, men and women have very different ways of communicating. Men often use verbal banter that can sound a bit harsh for women. They can call one another names, tease one another, and even play crude jokes on one another. They can go to extremes that seem almost offensive to women. And if they start to treat us like one of the boys, we can often misinterpret their communication approach and get our feelings hurt. And we don't always know how to respond.

Women have several linguistic patterns that can create problems of misinterpretation for us as well. Let me outline some for you.

- **Disclaimers** – These are the phrases we often use before speaking or writing our main message. Familiar disclaimers are things like, "This may be a stupid question," or "This may not be relevant," or "I'm not sure if I should bring this up," and the list goes on. These disclaimers distract from our intended messages, our contributions, our points of view, and our ideas. They reflect a lack of confidence in what we're about to say. When you find yourself thinking or about to write such a disclaimer, avoid it and get to the point.

- **Hedges** – These are words that send a signal of wishy-washy communications. Hedges are words like "probably" or "sort of" or "maybe." I've even noticed newswomen using hedges when interviewing someone, which is in contrast to the teleprompter news they read. Listen for these hedges. The first place you can make changes is in your writing. Reread your emails or presentation scripts and work to eliminate the wishy-washy language.

- **Tag Questions** – These are questions we ask after making a point, offering a suggestion, or presenting an idea/solution/recommendation. Examples are "Does that make sense?" (one of my favorites) or "Wouldn't you agree?" Men often hear these tag questions as a need for their affirmation. Again, these convey a lack of confidence in what we're trying to communicate.

- **"I'm Sorry . . ."** – Think about this. Have you written an email in the last thirty days that started with, "I'm sorry it's taken me so long to get back to you"? And now think again. How many emails have you received from a male that start out that way? Don't get me wrong, if you *have* done something wrong, apologize for it and be specific about what you're sorry for. And yes, I know we are sorry when something bad happens to someone else. At the same time, I've heard a woman apologize just for stepping into the elevator. I have even noticed my granddaughter starting to use the "I'm sorry" phrase in a general way. And again, start with your written communications. Lead with your message. Lose the "I'm sorry."

- **"Should"** – I think this is one of the most debilitating words we can speak. We "should" on ourselves all the time. "I 'should' have thought of that. I 'should' have said no. I really "should" lose those twenty "pounds." A colleague in my master's program shared this thought, "'Should' is 'could' with shame on it." Oh my gosh! That stopped me in my tracks. We really are shaming ourselves and others on a regular basis. So, stop "shoulding" on yourself.

  I also want to share another side of this. When someone is telling me what I "should" do, I often turn into my five-year-old self and think, "You're not the boss of me!" Now let's be real. That is about me—not the other person. It is what we often describe as a "trigger word." It sparks negative thoughts and feelings in me. And here is how I have learned not to give my power away to the other person—either by judging them or letting them put me in a feisty mood. I translate "should" to "could," and now I can stay engaged with the other person rather than being distracted by the language.

- **Sacrifice Versus Choice** – I hear women talk about sacrificing on a pretty regular basis. I encourage women to consider that they're making choices rather than sacrifices. In reality, all decisions we make have trade-offs. We are typically giving up something to get another thing of greater value. "I sacrifice time with my family because I work a full-time job." I can convert that to "I work full time so that I can provide financial support for my family, and that enables our family to send our children to good schools and to contribute to worthy causes that help my community." When I convert my own thinking and self-talk to one of choice, it is more empowering. Did you give up something (sacrifice)? Yes. Did you get something greater? Yes (family standard of living and financial security). One is about scarcity; the other is about abundance. One is about guilt, and the other is about empowerment.

- **"I Will" Versus "I Will Try"** – Numerous studies have asked men versus women to describe something that they would want at some future state. Men use the language of "I will" as if they have already accomplished it. Women use tentative language of "I hope to" or "I will try to." We all know that men have no better idea or certainty that they will achieve this future state, and yet they sound more confident and assured in their language. For women it is often a matter of honesty. I encourage you to give yourself credit for all the things you have never done yet figured out how to get done. All the things you thought you couldn't do and were surprised you could do once you tried— perhaps some were much easier than you imagined they would be! All of us have gone into unknown situations, done our research, diagnosed the key issues, and built solutions to solve for a desired outcome.

Come on, ladies, we've got this. Let's trust ourselves to be learners, to be resilient, to figure it out, and to make it happen!

GOAL-ORIENTED VERSUS PROCESS-ORIENTED

When you ask a woman a question or if a woman is making a presentation or reviewing a slide "deck" with her boss, she is likely to do extensive setting up. She might explain the many options she considered before she landed on the one she chose. By the time she gets to the real point in her presentation, she could be on slide number twenty-five—and has lost the attention of her boss or other audience.

Women want to take you through the process before giving you the answer. We can find ourselves being viewed as poor communicators because we can't get to the point. Now let's be real, women are goal-oriented, we just want to make sure the other person knows that we have done our homework, and our proposal or recommendation is credible based on the great (and tedious!) work we've done to arrive at our answer. I also wonder if we like to describe our process because we don't feel we get the credit we deserve for the work we do, or that it is so hard to get a word in that when we finally get the floor, we want to hold on to it. No research on that—more my anecdotal experience and curiosity.

Men often prefer to hear the answer first and then will ask questions requiring you to then give the backstory or the process of how you've arrived at your recommendation. Therefore, if I am presenting to a man, I want the bottom-line answer to be there by at least slide number five or within the first five minutes of the conversation or presentation. What I've learned is that men can't hear you until they get the answer. They tune you out, interrupt you, or discount what you eventually bring based on their need to get to the answer.

My husband taught me a lesson early on by saying to me, "Marsha, this is a yes-or-no question." This was long before I started studying gender differences. I slowed down, gave him the yes or no response, and he got what he needed. And because we had a mutually respectful kind of relationship, he then invited me to share how I got to my answer. We both respected the other's need to get what they needed from our communication, and it better ensured that our intended messages were being delivered, understood, and appreciated.

Because we tend to work and live in more masculine environments, many women have learned how to do the bottom-line presentation. So, pay attention to how both men and women like to receive information. More than gender is at play; consider whether I'm an introvert or an extrovert, how much time I have, the strength of our trust for one another, and how much I already know.

I was coaching a woman recently who was doing a strategic planning presentation to a vice president whom she supported. The meeting was cut short by the vice president because the presenters spent too much time on the setup. The presenters left that meeting, re-worked their presentation by getting to the key components of the plan much earlier, and then had a successful second meeting. If there are both men and women in your audience, determine, if possible, whether the final decision maker is male or female. Lean toward the gender tendencies of that final decision maker. And, if there are women in the room who are influencers, make sure you provide a bit of background and preparation to satisfy their tendencies to consider background and process.

MEETINGS

Men and women do meetings very differently. The concept of the "meeting before the meeting" plays a big role here. Many of us have learned the need for these premeetings over a long career. We may not even realize that we are doing these premeetings or why. Women may see it as unnecessary and a waste of time. Why can't we do our work and make decisions in the meeting?

Another consideration when we go into meetings where decisions are made or approvals are granted is that we have to be politically savvy. Okay, let's be honest. When I used the word "politically," did you feel a tightening? Women tend to see anything smacking of political as a negative and as a limiter for them. Let me differentiate between "being political" and being "politically savvy." Being political is about pushing your own agenda to the exclusion of others and often for personal gain. That is generally what turns women (and men) off, and we all know people who use this approach whenever trying to convince their audience of anything. This is not something we want driving our organizations, culture, or interactions.

Being politically savvy is about knowing how to navigate the organizational landscape in order to come up with a great solution. To be politically savvy, we must be clear about our positions and open to the input of others. Being politically savvy requires us to be aware of and manage the following four roles typically present in most decision-making or approvals:

- **Decision maker(s)** – Most big decisions have multiple decision makers, and they can be a mix of genders, come from different backgrounds, have varying styles, etc. We typically start at the bottom of the hierarchy getting our approvals or buy-in. Craft your messages and approach based on the decision maker. As a woman in one of my classes stated, "Never take 'no' as an answer from someone who is not the final decision maker." In other words, try again (resiliency) with that lower-level decision maker, or escalate to the next level (courage) with transparency to the person who gave you the "no."

- **Allies** – These are people who agree with your ideas, approach, recommendations, or solutions. To know that someone is my ally is not enough. I want to have that meeting before the meeting with them and ask for their vocal public support. Don't assume they will do that. Ask specifically for what you want.

- **Adversaries** – These are people who will likely recommend or propose something very different from you. As women, we often avoid these meetings before the meeting, or even avoid the person altogether. This is a dangerous thing for us to do. We need to meet with them almost more than anyone. We have to know their position and be prepared to neutralize it. In reality, I have found that the resistance I conjured up in my head was far worse than the reality of the actual meeting and discussion. Ideally, you will be able to find a few areas or topics on which you're in agreement. Acknowledge and appreciate that and then take those things off the table. Are there other items where you can negotiate or compromise? (For example, if we agree to use your software application, will you give me the person on your team who can help us implement it successfully for this client? I give you your desired software package and you give me a skilled and experienced resource to implement it.)

- **Gatekeepers** – These are the people who can give or deny you access—to people and their calendars for the meetings before the meeting, or to information you need to build your business case. Gatekeepers can be executive assistants, chiefs of staff, financial analysts, or subject-matter experts. This is a large group and reinforces our need to be on good terms with everyone, because you never know when you'll need what they can provide. And if you find yourself in a gatekeeper role, be thoughtful in responding to requests for time, people, or information.

The next area I want to discuss is how meeting communication occurs. Men tend to talk in meetings 70 percent of the time. Men speak at length because they want you to know how much they believe in what they're saying or recommending. This figure has been corroborated by several studies. And this is no matter how many men versus women are in the meeting. A study from Harvard shows that the larger the group, the more likely men are to speak. Women often lament that it is so hard to get their voice in the room, to be heard in meetings where men are "mansplaining" or dominating the airtime. (Mansplain: "to explain something to a woman in a condescending way that assumes she has no knowledge about the topic," Merriam-Webster.com, *Merriam-Webster*, https://www.merriam-webster.com/dictionary/mansplain.)

Women also describe experiences of saying something and it being ignored; then, a few minutes later a man says the same thing and it is heard and discussed or considered. Someone once sent me a cartoon with a group of men sitting around a table with one woman at the table. The man standing at the head of the table is saying, "That's a wonderful point, Mrs. Trigg. Perhaps if one of the men said it, we could hear it." Yet another program participant told me that, in her company, the act of repeating a woman's idea only moments after she expressed it was termed a "he-peat."

If we give up and stop trying to contribute, men perceive our silence as: "She can't keep up, she isn't smart enough to understand, or she has nothing to contribute." Sound familiar?

GETTING MY VOICE IN THE ROOM

In meetings, women tend to raise their hands to make a contribution or ask a question, and this can result in getting ignored. Men, on the other hand, feel comfortable interrupting, and thereby improve their chances of taking command of the conversation or topic. We have to learn to *keep right on talking* when men interrupt us. When we do keep talking—undaunted and unfazed—others will stop talking because they know we're not giving up the floor.

Of course, this sort of "defiance" goes against everything in us. In fact, women regularly shush one another in the name of "manners," chastising *one another* for interrupting—most recently, a colleague filled me in on how her own sister, a corporate guru in a billion-dollar company known for its "culture" (where employees are encouraged to "work on themselves"), repeatedly calls her out on interrupting, to the point that my colleague can rarely get a word in edgewise without causing some sort of strife.

In the quest of teaching us to be "good girls," our very role models and teachers—and even family members—have taught us not to interrupt, and to defer to others. We learned this in our early school days, and we are still learning it in our professional lives. Even when teachers are made aware that they call on boys significantly more than girls, the trend of giving priority to the male voices continues.

As far as the roles men can play, they need to learn how to create a more inclusive meeting environment, where all voices can be heard and their contributions considered. For women, we have to give up some of our "good girl" behaviors in order to be heard. And women, we *can* help one another out.

There is a concept called "amplification." I first read about it as something that the women in President Obama's press room did to support one another and to neutralize men talking 70 percent of the time in their meetings. When a woman offered her point of view or was trying to intervene to make a point, another woman or women would reinforce or amplify the point she was making. Some of the more assertive women would help create a break in the conversation to allow the woman to contribute her thought or idea. That is a beautiful example of women supporting women!

And women, we need to be aware of when we interrupt or cut other women off. We're not helping ourselves when we display such behavior.

SUCCESS AND FAILURE

Here is yet another practice that most of us can relate to. When a woman receives a compliment or word of recognition, she tends to deflect it or minimize it. Someone tells us they like our blouse. We devalue their words, responding, "Oh, this old thing; I got it on sale." Or someone tells us we've done a great job leading a project to a successful conclusion. We deflect, responding, "Oh, it wasn't me; it was my team." This is one thing that we can begin to change immediately. To deflect or devalue the praise is to diminish ourselves. I think of this in terms of a mathematical equation: Results + Recognition = Power/Influence.

Every woman who has ever been in my programs is there because she has gotten results. These are typically high-achieving, high-potential women who have been nominated to be in the program. And yet, they often deny their achievements and are shocked that they were considered to be in the program. They also tell story after story about how this denial shows up in their day-to-day lives as well.

Many of us have been taught to just say "thank you" when offered a compliment or some kind of praise. I want you to go a step further. I encourage you to say something along the lines of, "Thank you. I'm proud of the leadership I provided, and I have a great team to work with." I call this the "I + We" approach. I am not taking all the credit nor am I deflecting the credit. The truth is I couldn't have done it without them, and likely they could not have done it without me. The teaching point is this: *When we take ourselves out of the success story, we're giving everyone else permission to do the same.* Take a moment and let that sink in—reread that last sentence. It is not arrogant. It is not bragging. It is acknowledging and accepting that my contributions mattered.

Men will often respond quite differently. They assume they will succeed and are quite willing to take the credit for the success. This isn't good or bad—it is simply a different approach. We can learn a lesson from them.

Dr. Heim describes a cartoon that someone sent her where a woman is standing up in front of a mirror trying to zip up her pants. She declares, "I've got to go on a diet." The next frame is a man standing in front of a mirror also trying to get his pants zipped up. He declares, "Something is wrong with these pants."

NONVERBAL CUES

Men and women have different abilities when it comes to noticing and interpreting nonverbal cues. Some studies done using a PET scan, which uses electrodes on your head to measure your brain activity, have arrived at this conclusion. The part of the brain that shows red is active, the part of the brain that shows blue is inactive, and an array of colors is in between the two.

The researchers show a man ten pictures of people's faces reflecting different emotions, and they ask him to name each emotion. His brain lights up all over—but he gets most of the answers wrong. In other words, his brain is working really hard, yet he still doesn't get the answer right. Then the researchers show a woman the same ten pictures. There is a small red spot on the PET scan and she gets most of them right. She is adept at reading nonverbal cues, and it doesn't take a lot of effort.

Empathy is typically higher in women, and that's what allows us to better read the nonverbal cues. It is also what serves us well as mothers to read our children's cues (e.g., that look means "I'm hungry," "I'm wet," or "I need to be cuddled"). I was called the "secret weapon," as salesmen would take me on sales calls—not to present or sell, but rather to read the room and let them know who was buying the pitch or not. That is an example of me playing to my gifts and the organization playing to them as well.

Another nonverbal cue that can cause us problems is nodding. Women nod to communicate that we hear you, we're interested, and we're following along. Men nod in agreement. So, when a man sees a woman nodding, he assumes that she agrees with him, and that may or may not be true. If we nod and then come back to the man with a different response, he often feels blindsided or may see us as wishy-washy. I am cognizant when meeting with a man not to nod unless I truly mean "yes," because I don't want to send an unintended or confusing signal of agreement.

BODY ORIENTATION

Even how men and women stand in relation to others is different. Women tend to stand face-to-face, looking at the other person's face.

(Remember the study regarding the first twenty-four hours and the pink blanket?) For women, this is an engaged body orientation. Men tend to stand side by side, shoulder to shoulder and looking out. Women often read this as "he is not listening or doesn't much care about what I have to say." In reality, men interpret the female face-to-face with hands on hips stance as aggressive.

In addition, we often try to adjust to feel comfortable in our preferred body orientation. I start out side by side with a man and keep turning to make face-to-face contact, and he keeps turning, as if we're in a circular dance. The coaching tip here is to stay planted and let the other person adjust to a comfortable orientation to you, and don't misinterpret their body orientation as anything other than a difference. In other words, don't dismiss a man's posture as being disengaged or ineffective.

Women have told me that, after learning about these body orientation differences, they have started sitting beside their significant other when having important conversations. Maybe it is on the couch, taking a walk, or even in the car. They have cited better results and a more engaging conversation.

REFLECTION:

Which of these "Invisible Differences" ring true for you?

How do these behaviors or differences work for you? Work against you? (Think about both your personal and professional world.)

What changes might you make when working across gender lines to deliver your intended messages or express your confidence in your abilities?

THE FEMALE AND MALE BRAINS

The female brain . . . why should it matter to us? The information I'm sharing here is from Dr. Louann Brizendine's research. She is the author of *The Female Brain* and *The Male Brain*. With new developments in neuroscience, we now recognize the importance of understanding how the female brain changes during life stages, including puberty, motherhood, and menopause. Our female brains react differently to the world around us than male brains do, including marketing and product promotion. How we interact in groups, and even the purpose of the interactions themselves, is different. An awareness of how the female brain works, relative to the male brain, creates an understanding of how your brain could personally impact you and your colleagues, and what you can do to prepare for that.

I have tried to describe these differences between genders in a practical way. There will be some sophisticated labeling for different parts of our brains and what each of those parts does. My hope is to offer you the practical application of knowing this information so that you may benefit from it. I also want to acknowledge that we are learning more about our brains every day. In addition, we're learning about the role that our hormones play in our thinking and feeling as well. Here we go!

THE FEMALE BRAIN

The female brain is 9 percent smaller than the male brain and is packed more tightly. This does not mean we have less brainpower. It is merely a fact based on our skull size. As a result, our brains are more densely constructed, and this helps explain some of the differences of brain processing.

The female brain has more neural connections going from side to side, from the left lobe to the right lobe, which accounts for increased intuition and communication skills. Little girls often develop stronger communication skills than little boys, and at an earlier age. The male brain has more connections front to back within the same hemispheres, which accounts for their increased spatial skills and muscular control.

In females, the prefrontal cortex is larger. This is the brain's center for language (communication) and observing emotions (empathy and nonverbal cues) and has 11 percent more neurons than the male brain. Our circuitry is wired for safety and fear and activates far more than male brains in anticipation of fear or pain. Women are smarter about risk-taking and contingency planning because our hippocampus, where emotions and memory are stored, is larger. It helps us remember what works and what doesn't work and, therefore, plan accordingly. (It's also why we tend to hold grudges longer.)

In the beginning, a woman in the ancient world shopped. She gathered fruits, berries, and herbs, and had to know where to find the best ones. She identified those special spots, because others depended on her to do so for their very survival. She had a built-in ability to focus on caring for others.

The wiring to nurture and protect lends itself to our "flat-power structure" and "power dead-even" approach to interpersonal relationships—forming alliances and seeking intimacy. Social harmony is crucial for the female brain. In nonverbal communication, females are strongly empathetic and score higher on emotion-recognition tests than men. This brain research corroborates Dr. Heim's research that we shared earlier.

The research on language differences across genders is another topic that continues to evolve. Women using three times more words than men on a daily basis have been cited in various literature sources in the past twenty-five years. More recent research has shown changes in the almost three-to-one ratio of words used by women versus men. These recent studies show varying results. In some cases women use more words than men. In other cases, men talk more than women. And in yet other cases, men and women talk about the same amount. The more recent research also notes that many variables other than gender account for the differences. For example, the amount of positional power one has, whether someone is introverted or extroverted, and both organization and country culture. I will be curious about how this topic is described in future studies. In the context of this book, my wish is for women to speak up when they have a point of view, a good idea, or a meaningful contribution to make.

THE MALE BRAIN

The male brain has evolved to procreate and protect. He is wired to form alliances that will allow him to provide for his family. The male's brain center for anger, fear, and aggression is larger than ours. The ventral tegmental area, the motivation center in all humans, is more active in the male brain than the female brain, and the medial preoptic area, where our sex drive lives, takes two and a half times more brain space in the male brain than the female brain. (Oh, that explains a lot.)

In the beginning, the ancient man hunted. He left the tribe for days at a time to stealthily seek and kill game. He has a built-in ability to focus on solving problems. The wiring to "protect" lends itself to the dominance, competitive, even hierarchical approach.

Protecting the family is somewhat akin to protecting his business, so it would make sense that he is competitive at the core—winning is something that matters, when the stakes are high. Males score higher on spatial skill tests and have great control over their large muscles earlier than females.

PUBERTY

During puberty, her brain sprouts, reorganizes, and prunes neuronal circuits. She is struggling for independence and identity and connects through talking. Her once stable brain now experiences hormonal fluctuations through a monthly cycle. Her primary interest is in finding a mate, love, and career development.

For males, his brain experiences a twenty-fold increase in testosterone during puberty, with a jump in vasopressin as well. He avoids his parents and challenges authority. As a young adult, his primary interest is on finding sexual partners and focusing on his job, money, and career development.

THE MOMMY BRAIN AND THE DADDY BRAIN

Then comes the "mommy" brain and the "daddy" brain. Moms-to-be are sleepier and need to rest and eat more. Predictability is the key to keep the mommy brain calm and focused.

Neurogenesis, which consists of the creation of new neurons, changes portions of her brain, and these portions will remain altered for the rest of her life. The mommy brain is laying down superhighways of neural connections that are continually reinforced by spending time with the baby. The effect of giving birth on a new mother's brain is immediate and powerful.

About four to six weeks after discovering they are going to be fathers, the daddy brain experiences a surge of distress. As their partner's pregnancy progresses, men's hormones also change. During the last trimester of pregnancy, men's prolactin levels can increase by over 20 percent, and testosterone drops by 13 percent. After the baby is born, the father's newly adjusted hormones help him bond emotionally with the baby and even increase his ability to hear the baby's cries. As the child grows, the daddy brain engaging in play becomes a crucial part of the child's development.

AT WORK

The female brain's social sensitivity is significant in a team's performance, and women tend to score higher in this arena than men. Placing a greater number of women on teams can increase a group's emotional intelligence.

Females tend not only to express their emotions more openly, but also to exaggerate the emotions they are experiencing empathetically from others. Companies who have three or more women in executive leadership are statistically far more successful.

In male brains, the circuitry is highly specialized to quickly process emotions to get to a "fix-it-fast" solution. In the context of team performance, his type of fix often involves less use of collaboration—or collaboration that doesn't run as deep in terms of social sensitivity. Males master the "guy face"—an expression that is allowed to reflect only confidence and strength . . . never fear or doubt.

LATER IN LIFE

For women, perimenopause occurs two to nine years before menopause, starting when a woman is about forty-three years old. At about forty-seven years old, the female brain experiences daily uncertainty due to erratic amounts of estrogen. Women in this phase can experience fluctuating interest in sex, erratic sleep patterns, and end up fatigued and easily irritated.

Midlife manhood looks remarkably like his twenties and thirties did. Men retain their ability to father children for life and do not experience the hormonal shifts as significantly as women do when they enter their forties and fifties. For the male brain, the urges to protect their turf, demonstrate aggression, take risks, and continue to ascend the ladder of career success are all still very important.

REFLECTION:

What stands out for you about the differences in the female and male brains?

What new insights did you gain?

How does this information help you better know yourself?

IMPOSTOR PHENOMENON

Research originally presented by Dr. Pauline Rose Clance and her colleague, psychotherapist Dr. Suzanne Imes, in a 1978 article entitled "The Impostor Phenomenon in High Achieving Women" argues that many of us, to varying degrees, exhibit feelings of being "an impostor" in our own lives. Doctors Clance and Imes discovered, in working with high-achieving women, that the women exhibited a significant pattern of dismissing accomplishments as some kind of fluke.

These women were incapable of internalizing positive feedback or external data that clearly indicated their high levels of achievement, talent, and intelligence, instead believing that they had somehow "fooled" other people or the system.

Impostor phenomenon (IP) sufferers live in a state of wondering, "When will I be found out?" and frequently visualize the horrific consequences of being discovered. It's an internal experience by individuals who consistently demonstrate a high level of achievement, yet feel incompetent and fear failure in relation to their perceived fraudulent success. Women who suffer from IP fail to incorporate their competencies into their identities. They perpetually engage in self-doubt and ritualistic worry of being exposed to others as less capable than they actually are.

THE IMPOSTOR CYCLE

Chart developed by Tracie Shipman based on the work of Dr. Pauline Clance.

The Impostor Cycle begins as a **NEW OPPORTUNITY** that is presented to the IP sufferer, and she enters the **Joy/Good Feelings** stage. Remember, she is a high-achieving performer who is recognized by others for her competencies, so she frequently receives offers to work on new projects—especially projects that stretch her! Once the request to step up comes in, she walks around the circle to the initial positive feelings of joy, maybe even euphoria, and the thoughts swirling in the back of her mind center on how nice it is to be recognized for her previous hard work and that "this time, it will be great!"—"it" being the result, the process, or whatever else seems to need redemption from the last project.

Which leads us to the second turn in the cycle—**Redemption/ Determination**. For the chronic IP sufferer, projects eventually morph into mini opportunities to continually redeem oneself. The link between work and self-worth for IP sufferers is strong. A feeling of determination sets in as she decides to accept the offer to work on the new opportunity, leaning into the good feelings with a sense that *this time* will finally be the one where she "proves" (to whatever imaginary jury lives in her head) that she is worthy of all this external praise and recognition. The kicker is that these beliefs about redemption and proof are buried deep in her subconscious, and she is operating completely unaware that her acceptance of the project is driven by these deep, unclarified, and unspoken needs.

Sadly, the positive feelings associated with accepting a new opportunity are typically short-lived—lasting perhaps only a few minutes. Once the drive for redemption kicks in, any joy associated with the project is fleeting. The IP sufferer's thoughts and feelings shift from joy and determination to doubt and dread, reinforced by internal beliefs such as, "I never should have accepted this assignment," "What was I thinking?" and "This was a mistake. I'll never be able to re-create the last success!"

Since so much of what is going on for IP sufferers lies beneath the surface of their awareness, lurking in the subconscious, the source of any feelings of worry and fear are often masked or even completely hidden. The IP sufferer is completely unaware that she is suffering because of IP—she just knows she is suffering. The tape of doubt and dread has been running in her head for so long that it is unrecognizable as the source of her suffering.

Enter the bad-dreams phase of the Impostor Cycle! If the IP sufferer isn't consciously aware that her feelings of worry and fear are tied to IP, her subconscious will use dreams to sort through her fears. Depending on the level of distress going on surrounding a particular project, the intensity of the bad dreams will vary. Many IP sufferers have shared that their dreams evolve from mildly frustrating (repeated dreams of losing things, showing up unprepared for something important, getting lost) to truly terrifying (catastrophic plane crashes, loved ones dying due to their mistake or negligence, apocalyptic disasters). The good news is, and *yes, there is good news*, that once an IP sufferer is aware of the IP Cycle, they can actually use the bad dreams as a "wake-up call" to recognize that they have entered into the cycle. They can then begin to address and mitigate the pain and suffering.

The **Bad Dreams, Worry, Fear** phase often partners with the **Immobility/Procrastination** phase, creating a dance of dread that freezes IP sufferers in place. Once thoughts like "I should have never said yes" or "I don't know what I'm doing" start rolling in the background, the protective systems of the brain kick into survival mode—because the NEW OPPORTUNITY now represents a threat or danger to our IP friend, and her brain, in protective mode, fights, flees, or freezes. Unless the IP sufferer develops an awareness that her IP is the culprit, she uses her protective mechanisms to move away from the dangerous opportunity (aka, *the project*).

The creative lengths to which an IP sufferer will immobilize or procrastinate (which could entail either freezing or fleeing) to avoid *the project* are legendary. Stories of everything from massive office deep cleaning to closet reorganizations to complete construction projects have been shared by chronic IP sufferers—all as strategies for avoiding the feared project that will surely bring about their inevitable fall from grace.

The length of the Immobility/Procrastination phase varies from project to project and person to person. However, one consistency is that there seems to be a magical switch that flips for chronic IP sufferers—a switch that tells the brain, "Okay, you really need to get your act together and start working on *the project* because your reputation is at stake and you promised," while ALSO whispering, "Oh, and since you waited so long and have created this ridiculous time crunch to deliver on your promises, you now have a BUILT-IN EXCUSE in case it turns out badly!"

Therein lies the superstitious aspect of the IP Cycle that reinforces the vicious loop of destructive thinking and behaviors. Procrastination leads to **Frenzied Work,** which, surprisingly, still manages to produce outstanding results and SUCCESS from our high-achieving performer! It's that mini-loop of cause and effect, *wait until the last minute then frenzied output = outstanding results,* that feels like the formula for success, so, in the subconscious mind of the IP sufferer, to alter that formula might lead to disaster. The Immobilization/Procrastination phase *feels like* an important step in the process and, if omitted, might not yield the same successful outcomes. Even when an IP sufferer is made aware of their procrastination, they often justify it as part of a "creative process" or being an "adrenaline junkie" who thrives on the energy of last-minute deadlines—even when the deadline was in place weeks or months ago.

One might assume that the IP Cycle would end with the SUCCESS of any given project, but the destructive nature of the cycle continues to linger and further toxify the thoughts and feelings of the IP sufferer.

Once a deadline is met, deliverables are handed off, and the project is officially declared a SUCCESS, an immediate sense of relief washes over the IP sufferer. There may even be some celebratory joy connected with the end, but it's mostly just a huge mental sigh—once again they managed to survive their mostly self-imposed turmoil. The temporary nature of the relief is directly related to how quickly the next phase kicks in—a review of their **"Tiny Failure" Inventory List.**

Some chronic IP sufferers have been preemptively tracking their failures throughout the project, so that when the shoe inevitably drops at the end and they are discovered to be a fraud, they can at least be prepared with their own list of the many reasons why. (Remember, they have been saving their built-in procrastination excuse for this very moment.) The "Tiny Failure" Inventory List is NOT about placing blame on others! The IP sufferer completely and totally OWNS every one of their errors.

This is a list of *every mistake made along the way* in the course of the project—even the mistakes the IP sufferer corrected "but shouldn't have made in the first place." It also includes the "if onlys." "If only I knew more about the topic/process/software," or "If only I had collaborated more with so and so," and, ironically, "If only I had given myself more time."

What is perhaps most remarkable about the "Tiny Failure" Inventory List is that it also includes peripheral errors—mistakes that had nothing to do with the actual project but are linked, nonetheless, in the IP sufferer's mind to the project. These errors are often connected to "all the other things" in the woman's life that she didn't accomplish (to whatever level of standards she set for herself) *while working on the project*! So the project results were outstanding, BUT . . .

- She didn't volunteer to be a field-trip chaperone during the deadline.

- She ate nothing but carbs during her "frenzied work" and gained two pounds.

- She missed acknowledging her friends' birthdays on social media.

- Her kids ate fish sticks and boxed macaroni and cheese . . . three times!

At this point, women who have little to no IP chatter in their heads often respond to the "Tiny Failure" Inventory List in utter disbelief. They cannot imagine someone so externally competent, so put together and successful, battling those internal negative, self-defeating thoughts. Yet, time after time, chronic IP sufferers are overwhelmed in a wash of emotion as they recognize themselves as stuck in this cycle. They see, often for the first time, how self-defeating and debilitating their beliefs truly are.

One of the biggest challenges for women who DO NOT have high IP symptoms is dealing with the women they know and respect who

DO have high IP symptoms. Their first instinct is usually to respond with encouraging, supportive feedback, "But you're so awesome. You've accomplished so much. You're a freaking rock star!" and then they proceed to provide their "evidence." To the innocent bystander, these words of support might sound completely appropriate and even therapeutic. However, to the IP sufferer, these words usually provide little to no succor, and, surprisingly, can sometimes create an even deeper spiral of self-doubt and shame.

Chronic IP sufferers have a heightened love/hate relationship with the next phase in the IP Cycle—**External Feedback: Discount ANY Praise**. External feedback is simply any information that comes in from an outside source—be it individuals or data. Timely, high-quality feedback is essential for the success of most projects. Unfortunately, IP sufferers filter feedback in an atypical way. Negative feedback that reinforces or adds to their already growing "Tiny Failure" Inventory List is filed away as valid. Such negative feedback is processed and accepted as perpetually accurate and then attached to their story about themselves—*not as an attribute of the project*, but as a characteristic of their own capability.

Naturally, if the negative feedback is mostly if not completely true, then it only makes sense that any possible positive praise must be discounted, or denied as invalid. Feedback that is positive in nature, including actual achievements like degrees, certifications, and awards, is easily diminished in the mind of the IP sufferer as being tied to hard work, timing, luck, connections, etc., but is not intrinsically linked to their own worth. For the IP sufferer, positive feedback or praise feels like a quickly melting snowflake that lands on their heavy woolen coat woven from the fibers of their "Tiny Failure" Inventory List. They see it fall, land, and then melt—an exquisite but temporary moment of joy.

This discounting of praise often stems from early life experiences. The source of this distrust of praise can usually be traced to those well-meaning adults who managed to, unwittingly, develop dark and twisted connections between praise and reality. For some women, this disconnect comes from their youth, in the form of adults who were overly enthusiastic with their encouragement and elevated every little achievement. Likely, our high-achieving woman was an equally high-achieving child who recognized that not every drawing or cartwheel was "amazing" and "the best ever." This recognition of reality versus praise left her with a gnawing sense of unease. When people praised her, it wasn't always true. Yet, when her errors or faults were pointed out by others—a spelling mistake, her inability to get the basketball through the hoop, singing off-key—she was keenly aware that the feedback received from others MATCHED her own internal experience. She could see or hear for herself that she was missing the mark.

On the other end of the scarce spectrum, some women grew up in environments where positive feedback consisted of meager, miserly amounts of praise doled out by her elders in spite of abundant evidence of high achievement. For these women, the measuring stick for what is "praiseworthy" is so high that praise for anything that doesn't measure up is perhaps lovely but certainly not credible—and therefore irrelevant.

Discounting praise is strongly related to another characteristic of women with IP where they deny their strengths or competencies. This self-denial is linked to the next phase in the IP Cycle, **Exaggerate Criticism/Deny Success.** Women who struggle with high IP often believe:

- "Whatever I'm weak in is what constitutes real intelligence."

- "Doing what I'm good at doesn't count. What counts is doing what I find difficult or challenging."

- "When I inevitably find something hard to accomplish, I have renewed proof of my lack of intelligence."

The inability to recognize one's natural gifts and competencies makes it easy to discount achievements as one's own. Denying success is less about humility and more about believing in a false sense of self—a nightmarish fairy tale of the girl who couldn't or shouldn't have. Heaven forbid she be asked to repeat her magical feats, only to have the village discover her original powers were a fluke after she, of course, finally fails.

This fractured fairy tale of distorted beliefs leads the IP sufferer to retreat. The final phase of the IP Cycle is **Shrink Back/Lay Low**. Without realizing it, these high-achieving women protectively pull back from the pressure that inevitably (automatically, for her) comes with new opportunities. The reflexive action of shrinking back and laying low provides a much-needed respite from the drama and trauma of entering into another cycle—a cycle that is invisible and inescapable for IP sufferers. That is, until they know better!

WHY BE CONCERNED?

The anxiety, dread, and doubt prevent any enjoyment of personal successes. Those with IP can develop depression and adverse physical symptoms. They may begin seeking less challenging tasks, further diminishing their self-worth and the full development of any personal and positional power.

The fear of failure is so strong that, while a woman intellectually understands that everyone fails and that no one is perfect, she's unable to apply this reality to herself. She sets extremely high standards of performance, expecting herself to be productive, insightful, and creative ALL OF THE TIME. Going to great lengths to ensure no criticism comes their way, these women frame their thinking to believe that anything less than perfection is failure. Typically, women with IP attain "stardom" early in their formative years. Then, they discover that other "stars" exist and begin to discount their value because they are no longer THE best, but only ONE OF the best.

Not addressing IP issues can be devastating for individuals, both personally and professionally. It's also just as important that leaders recognize the detrimental impact IP can have on their teams and the organization as a whole. When teams have high-achieving members who are underperforming due to IP, the lost opportunity is significant . . . and could have been avoided entirely. Herein lies the personal tragedy!

Fortunately, both individuals with IP and their leaders can collaborate to develop a healthy, holistic plan for tackling IP beliefs and symptoms head-on. One of the first steps in the process for healing and stepping fully into all that high-achieving power is to identify which IP beliefs are in play and to what degree. The assessment that follows is a great start!

IMPOSTOR PHENOMENON SELF-ASSESSMENT

Very few people who are indeed experiencing the impostor phenomenon would label themselves as "impostors." Knowing that, Dr. Clance developed the Impostor Test© to help individuals determine whether or not they have IP characteristics and, if so, to what extent they are suffering.

Please answer the questions as honestly as possible. A rating of 1 means the statement is *not at all true*; a rating of 5 means the statement is *very true*; and an answer of 2, 3, or 4 represents the range where the statement may be true *rarely*, *sometimes*, or *often*.

It is best to give the first response that enters your mind rather than dwelling on each statement.

SELF-ASSESSMENT ACTIVITY:

1 = Not at All   2 = Rarely   3 = Sometimes   4 = Often   5 = Very True

_____ I have often succeeded on a test or a task even though I was afraid that I wouldn't do well before I undertook the task.

_____ I can give the impression that I'm more competent than I really am.

_____ I avoid evaluations if possible and have a dread of others evaluating me.

_____ When people praise me for something I've accomplished, I'm afraid I won't be able to live up to their expectations in the future.

_____ I sometimes think I obtained my present position or gained my present success because I happened to be in the right place at the right time or knew the right people.

_____ I'm afraid people important to me may find out that I'm not as capable as they think I am.

_____ I tend to remember the incidents in which I haven't done my best more than those times I have done my best.

_____ I rarely do a project or task as well as I'd like to do it.

_____ Sometimes I feel or believe that my success in my life or my job has been the result of some kind of error.

_____ It's hard for me to accept compliments or praise about my intelligence or accomplishments.

_____ At times, I feel my success has been due to some kind of luck.

_____ I'm disappointed at times in my present accomplishments and think I should have accomplished much more.

_____ Sometimes I'm afraid others will discover how much knowledge or ability I really lack.

_____ I'm often afraid that I may fail at a new assignment or undertaking even though I generally do well at what I attempt.

_____ When I've succeeded at something and received recognition for my accomplishments, I have doubts that I can keep repeating that success.

_____ If I receive a great deal of praise and recognition for something I've accomplished, I tend to discount the importance of what I've done.

_____ I often compare my ability to those around me and think they may be more intelligent than I am.

_____ I often worry about not succeeding with a project or on an examination, even though others around me have considerable confidence that I will do well.

_____ If I'm going to receive a promotion or gain recognition of some kind, I hesitate to tell others until it is an accomplished fact.

_____ I feel bad and discouraged if I'm not "the best" or at least "very special" in situations that involve achievement.

MY TOTAL SCORE: _____

SCORING YOUR ASSESSMENT

If your total score is 40 or less, you have few impostor characteristics. If you scored between 41 and 60, you have moderate IP experiences. A score between 61 and 80 means you frequently have impostor feelings. A score higher than 80 means you often have intense IP experiences.

We have referenced *high IP* often in this chapter, although we did not specify what we meant by *high*. While it might make sense that *high* could be anything above a score of 61, we intentionally leave the interpretation of *high* to those who take the assessment. For us, *high* is in the mind and heart of the beholder. What's more important than any hard and fast numeric marker is how deeply the descriptions of the Impostor Cycle and the assessment behaviors resonated with you and how much you intuitively connect them with your own experiences.

There is another lens through which we can view impostor phenomenon. A recent *Harvard Business Review* article called "Stop Telling Women They Have Impostor Syndrome," by Ruchika Tulshyan and Jodi-Ann Burey, was released February 11, 2021. The authors believe it's important "not to fix individuals, but to create an environment that fosters a number of different leadership styles and where diversity of racial, ethnic, and gender identities is viewed as just as professional as the current model."

I very much agree with their point. I don't think it is either/or; I think it is both/and. My view is that we're always thinking and working within the context of individual, interpersonal, team, organizational, and societal conditions/situations. The greatest changes can occur more quickly when we work at all levels. At certain times, the individual is the focus or is in the foreground, while the other four levels are operating in the background. At other times, the organization is in the foreground, while the other four are in the background. As a leader, you want to create a culture where everyone can bring their strengths and talents to the workplace, respecting the many different styles and ways of working to get things done.

MANAGING THE IMPOSTOR PHENOMENON

Once you have identified your degree of IP symptoms and how problematic they are (or aren't) for you, the next natural question for anyone who wants to reduce the impact of IP in their life is, "How can I decrease my impostor phenomenon feelings and reclaim my power?"

To be honest, when we first started on our journey over twenty years ago, Drs. Clance and Imes were the only ones in the field even talking about impostor phenomenon. Over the decades, more and more thought leaders have provided additional, fresh perspectives on the topic. Today, a simple Google, YouTube, or TEDTalk search will produce a cornucopia of theories on and remedies to the phenomenon or *syndrome*, as some call it today. Over the twenty-plus years that we have been studying and presenting IP to the women in our programs, we have collected what we believe to be the best of the best recommendations available, and we're sharing them with you here. They fall into three categories:

- Confronting IP Thoughts/Feelings

- Facing Fears

- Owning Strengths and Celebrating Success

CONFRONTING IP THOUGHTS/FEELINGS

First, know you are not alone. One of the most precious moments in our programs is when the women who have been silently suffering from IP look around the room at their competent peers and realize there are other women who feel just like they do. It's a power-filled, poignant moment for everyone. You may have friends or colleagues who, like you, have been holding on to these feelings but are afraid to share them—the very definition of someone with high IP. Be brave and be the first to bring up the topic. Maybe share the impostor phenomenon self-assessment with others in your circle and offer your score as an opening to the discussion. There is strength (and comfort) in numbers!

Focus on shifting one or two high IP scores at a time—over time. As high achievers, the reflexive reaction to "fixing this thing" may be to dive in and try to knock down all your 4s and 5s. However, it is important to have compassion for yourself through this process—realistically, the better approach is to look at one or two behaviors from the list of twenty and focus on those. What would you need to do and/or believe to go from "very true" or "often" to "sometimes"? Finding a mentor for a particular behavior can be a great way to explore new beliefs and thought patterns that could ultimately lead to a shift for you.

Actively practice true self-compassion. No one is doing the math here, but just in case, remember that you have been building these beliefs for quite a while—possibly even decades. Shifting deeply embedded beliefs will not happen overnight, and the new thought patterns won't necessarily stick immediately. Allow yourself the same learning curve, leeway, and patience that you offer others around you. Self-compassion is another hot topic on the internet, so it's pretty easy to find videos, podcasts, and other related materials centered entirely on that subject. Give yourself the gift of indulging in a study just for you.

Get curious when your inner critic takes over. It's quite possible that your inner critic has already been chattering in your ear about how dealing with this whole IP thing is going to be a problem and you probably ought to just ignore it. Some might tell you to shut out or ignore those negative thoughts, but we firmly believe there is value in acknowledging and honoring that voice, within boundaries.

Your inner critic is there for a reason and began as a mechanism to protect you from something or someone. It's for that reason that we suggest you DO listen to it.

- What is it saying?
- What could your inner critic be trying to protect you from?
- Where are these views coming from? When do you remember first hearing this?
- Why is it saying this?

- Why now?

Listen, leverage, and then let go. What can you *learn* from your inner critic? What is helpful? Once you've listened and leveraged the lessons of that voice, let it go with gratitude. These hints were culled from one of our favorite resources on the topic, from Dr. E. V. Estacio, titled *The Impostor Syndrome Remedy*.

Another addition to our IP Resource Library comes to us from Dr. Heidi Grant Halvorson and her work around the "Be Good vs. Getting Better Mindset." You can check out her entire video at https://www.youtube.com/watch?v=l4kz92qWpLA.

Dr. Halvorson's work helps IP sufferers calm their inner critic by understanding a crucial difference between "being good" and "getting better."

BEING GOOD	GETTING BETTER
Proving	Improving
Demonstrating Skills	Developing Skills
Performing Better Than Others	Performing Better Than I Have Before

FACING FEARS

Name your fear. Test it against reality. Since the biggest fear for most women with IP is that they will be "found out" as a fraud, simply unpacking the phenomenon itself with its accompanying cycle and symptoms from the assessment often provides immediate relief from that particular fear. Are you a fraud? Really? Unlikely! The data suggests otherwise. You wouldn't have a host of satisfied fans recruiting you for NEW OPPORTUNITIES if you were a fraud.

What is the fear driving your IP, if it's not about being a fraud? For some women, it's a confounding fear of showing up as "more than" the others around them—whether with their team, their boss, or their family. Women grow up with strong messages of equalizing or leveling themselves in comparison with others, messages along the lines of "Don't stand out . . . don't draw too much attention to yourself" or "Who does she think she is?"

The fear underneath your IP might be less about being a fraud and more about standing apart from or being separated from a group or an important individual who matters to you. If this resonates with you, there may be significant work for you to do in terms of recognizing your self-worth and confidence. If that is what is going on for you, it's a lot to unpack, undoubtedly. Again, a first step is to get clear on whether this possibility has any energy for you. Have you heard (and accepted) those diminishing warnings about playing small in the world?

One of our favorite inspirational "tools" to unlock this prison of playing small is this excerpt by Marianne Williamson titled, "Our Deepest Fear," from her book, *A Return to Love: Reflections on the Principles of "A Course in Miracles"*. It begins:

> Our deepest fear is not that we are inadequate.
> Our deepest fear is that we are powerful beyond measure.
> It is our light, not our darkness
> That most frightens us.
> We ask ourselves
> Who am I to be brilliant, gorgeous, talented, fabulous
> Actually, who are you not to be?

Marianne challenges us to consider that "playing small does not serve the world. There is nothing enlightened about shrinking so that other people won't feel insecure around you."

In addition to naming your fear and testing it against reality, another suggestion is to acknowledge the habitual aspect of your IP beliefs and begin the work necessary to shift to another thinking mode. Until now, you likely had no idea these IP beliefs existed, let alone understood how much they were driving your behaviors. But to paraphrase our dear teacher Maya Angelou, "Now that we know better . . . we can do better." As you notice the IP beliefs and patterns showing up in your day-to-day activities, you can stop, take a moment to check in with yourself, and then make a NEW CHOICE. To paraphrase another great teacher, Arya Stark, "What do we say to FEAR? Not today, FEAR, not today!"

(For those of you who aren't familiar with Arya Stark, she's a pivotal heroic character from the Game of Thrones series, written by George R. R. Martin.)

Build resiliency around making mistakes. One final strategy that we emphasize for facing fears is to increase our comfort level with failing. High-achieving women with IP have developed keen, ninja-like senses to sniff out the parts of projects that have "disaster" written all over them. This highly tuned radar usually "helps" them avoid obvious pitfalls. Then, to ensure they maintain their record of zero failures, they overprepare, overwork, and overdeliver. If, upon initial inspection, they don't believe they can meet their own extraordinary expectations on a project (or a promotion), they will seek a way to avoid it—either through procrastination, which we have already explored—or by stepping back from the NEW OPPORTUNITY altogether.

Living this way is exhausting! It not only keeps these high-achieving women from reaching their fullest potential professionally, but also sucks the joy out of anything they work on.

Of course, a first step to managing this is to "own it if you got it." Were you the student who didn't take a class unless you thought you could get an A in it? How is that mentality still driving your decisions and choices today?

Resiliency is its own big topic, so we won't dwell on it here. But one simple step to take to begin addressing this, as it relates to IP, is to once again lean in to the discomfort of not knowing or not being an expert at something and experiment—safely—with a new skill. Make it fun but challenging enough, with little risk of professional (or personal) injury if or when you fail. That's the key—choose something that you are pretty sure you have zero knowledge about or natural talent at so you will be guaranteed to struggle through the learning curve. Pick up a new sport, or a banjo, or a video game—something where you will get to feel complete frustration, yet you commit to stick with it anyway. Not because you're trying to be the best banjo player on the block (because that *will be* what your inner critic will start yammering about) but *because you want to learn how to live with and work through mistakes. Lots of them!* To build resilience, YOU MUST MAKE MISTAKES! There is no shortcut. Resilience is a capacity you build over time.

OWNING STRENGTHS AND CELEBRATING SUCCESS

Our last strategy for managing the impostor phenomenon centers on owning your strengths. The entire Power of Self Program is fundamentally built on the principle of becoming aware of and then owning our unique strengths, as women and as leaders. So while the concept is a cornerstone for the program, it is especially important to women who are struggling with IP.

Get crystal clear on your strengths and nonstrengths through assessments, feedback, and coaching. As the data comes in from these sources, look for themes and trends over time that help you form an accurate, unadulterated story of who you really are—centered on those strengths.

Remember that intelligence or competence is not a fixed state, but a changing and fluid never-ending process of growing and adapting. It's important for a woman with high IP to change her self-definition to one that focuses on and acknowledges the cumulative accomplishments she has achieved over her lifetime—her strengths, gifts, and core worth—without getting caught up in singular performance metrics tied to discrete tests, tasks, or tapped talents on any given day.

People around you, especially those who acknowledge and value your gifts and contributions, are going to try and tell you how awesome you are. Let them. Period.

When someone gives you positive feedback or praise, your response should be, "Thank you," rather than a dissertation on all the things you know went wrong or that you didn't do or how it "wasn't just me . . . it was the team."

Many women with high IP have become adept at pretending to accept praise—on the outside. But the internal dialogue continues to be a litany of confessional reasons why they don't truly deserve the praise. It's pretty hard to own our strengths and celebrate success when we won't allow any of the good stuff to filter in and hang out for more than a nanosecond. For that, we offer the following suggestion:

Recognize when you are discounting praise and, instead, truly allow it to soak in. Go beyond the professional niceties and allow yourself to listen and accept the praise—breaking the habit of hearing praise as some ritualistic reciprocity of empty gratitude shared among colleagues—in the true spirit it is given!

What if it's possible that those good things they are saying about you are TRUE?

Can you allow yourself to receive the gift of positive feedback being offered to you as an affirmation of your fundamental goodness? As an avalanche of praise-shaped snowflakes that cannot melt because you are allowing them to penetrate deep into your story of yourself—reshaping that story into something that is solid and strong and undeniable?

Will you dare to celebrate your unique gifts and successes with the same (or greater) energy and determination that you once used in order to keep yourself small?

Understanding how IP might be holding you back could be the key to unlocking your power![1]

---

1   Special thanks to Dr. Pauline Rose Clance for the material in this chapter. I drew much from her insightful book *The Impostor Phenomenon: Overcoming the Fear that Haunts Your Success* (Peachtree Publishers, Ltd., 1985) as well as from being a student when she and Dr. Imes taught this concept in our early programs.

CHAPTER 3

YOUR PERSONAL VISION

There are two ways of meeting difficulties. You alter the
difficulties or you alter yourself to meet them.

~ Phyllis Bottome

Many of us have developed or have been part of developing an organizational or team vision. Have you ever developed a personal vision? In a typical class of about thirty women, three to four women will raise their hands when I ask this question. Your vision represents the whole you—the personal and the professional. It prompts us to pause and envision what we want from our lives, beyond family responsibilities and obligations and beyond our career aspirations.

I am offering a structure with several inputs to help prepare you to write your personal vision: your values, your risk-taking propensity, your strengths, and a context for stretching your thinking to be fearless. Let's start with our values.

VALUES

Values are a set of principles or ideals that drive and guide a person's behavior. They reflect your judgment about what is important in your life. Understanding what your values are helps you to live a more authentic, happy, and purposeful life. They also give us a touch point for making decisions and setting priorities. Following are two lists of values—one personal and one professional. These are not intended to be exhaustive lists. Feel free to add what is important to you if you don't see it on the list. Remember, not everything can be a value. Values are those things we don't want to violate, that we will not compromise on.

ACTIVITY:

Place a check mark beside seven to ten values you rate most important in your life personally.

PERSONAL VALUES

___ Accomplishment	___ Financial Status	___ Power
___ Achievement	___ Health & Fitness	___ Recognition
___ Adventure	___ Helping Others	___ Reputation
___ Art	___ Hobbies	___ Respect
___ Available to My Children	___ Honesty	___ Romantic Relationships
___ Available to My Parents	___ Humor	___ Security
___ Community	___ Independence	___ Self-Improvement
___ Companionship	___ Justice	___ Sense of Control
___ Competitiveness	___ Leisure Time	___ Social Status
___ Creativity	___ Loyalty	___ Spiritual Growth
___ Education / Knowledge	___ Music	___ Sports
___ Ethics	___ Nature / Wildlife	___ Time Alone
___ Fairness	___ Neatness / Order	___ Travel
___ Fame	___ Peace of Mind	___ Volunteering
___ Family Relations	___ Personal Appearance	___ Wealth
___ Family Time	___ Pets	___ Worldview
___ Financial Comfort	___ Physical Challenge	

ACTIVITY:

Place a check mark beside seven to ten values you rate most important in your life professionally.

PROFESSIONAL VALUES

_____ Advancement–career progression

_____ Affiliation–member of an organization

_____ Authority–making decisions; supervising others

_____ Being Challenged– problem-solving; complex challenges

_____ Being Competitive– considered the best; winning

_____ Coaching–mentoring and developing others

_____ Developing Friendships– personal friends at work

_____ Earning High Income– significant compensation package

_____ Feeling of Community– working as part of a group or team

_____ Feeling Secure–low threat of job loss

_____ Global Perspective– global travel; transactions

_____ Helping Others– individually or in groups

_____ Helping Society–the world become a better place

_____ Independence–working autonomously

_____ Influencing Others– changing attitudes and opinions

_____ Learning–acquiring new knowledge

_____ Physically Active–freedom to move; be active

_____ Professional Status– garnering respect in my profession

_____ Providing Leadership– guiding, inspiring others

_____ Public Contact–working with and serving the public

_____ Variety–working on different things routinely

_____ Working Alone–little interaction with others

_____ Working at a Fast Pace– rapid-rate, high-paced activities and deadlines

_____ Working with Clients/ Patients–direct interactions

_____ Working with Ideas– creating new possibilities, innovating

_____ Working with My Hands–using hands to operate things

_____ Working with Numbers– analyzing, processing numbers

_____ Working with Words– written expression of ideas, products

Source: Adapted from the work of Rita Bailey, consultant and CEO of Boxages, LLC.

Now, let's combine these together. Thinking in terms of "Without these, I'm not me," let's align your personal and professional values by transferring those values you checked onto each list in the following table.

Personal Values	Professional Values

REFLECTION:

How are these values reflected in your life today . . . or not?

How do your personal and professional values align or not align?

How can these values inform your vision for your future and the commitment you're willing to make to achieve the vision you desire?

RISK-TAKING

One of the beliefs that has changed since starting this work some twenty years ago is that women are not risk-takers. More recent research has shown that women do, indeed, take risks. Because we also do contingency planning and, therefore, have a ready fallback position, it previously appeared that we didn't take risks. Dare I say, women may be smarter risk-takers. I love the following poem, as it speaks to me about the price of risk-taking.

To Risk

To laugh is to risk appearing the fool.
To weep is to risk appearing sentimental.
To reach out for another is to risk involvement.
To expose feelings is to risk exposing your true self.
To place your dreams before a crowd is to risk ridicule.
To love is to risk not being loved in return.
To live is to risk dying.
To hope is to risk despair.
To go forward in the face of odds is to risk failure.
But to risk we must, because the greatest hazard
in life is to risk nothing.
The person who risks nothing is one who does nothing,
has nothing, is nothing.
He may avoid suffering and sorrows,
but he cannot learn, feel, change, grow, or love.
Chained by her certitudes, she is a slave.
She has forfeited her freedom.
Only a person who takes risks is free.

–William Arthur Ward

There are always two sides to every choice we make. In this case, are you willing to put yourself out there and risk seeing the possible darker or less-than-ideal outcome of your choice? In one of my favorite quotes by Eleanor Roosevelt, we are told, "You gain strength, courage, and confidence by every experience in which you really stop to look fear in the face. You must do the thing which you think you cannot do." Yes, there is always a dark side, and I choose to see the positive in the possibilities when gauging whether I dare step up or step out.

REFLECTION:

How could taking more risks give you more freedom?

What are your thoughts and feelings after reading this poem and this quote? Does it challenge you? Inspire you?

How might this information contribute to your personal vision?

So, how much risk do you take? Thinking about your behavior over the last ninety days, place a check mark in the low, medium, or high column based on your own experience. Admittedly, risk can take many forms. Following is another list that is merely meant to help you identify what your risk propensity might be.

PERSONAL RISK

STATEMENT	LOW	MED	HIGH
I am willing to try new behaviors.			
I have recently shared radically new ideas with my peers and colleagues.			
I take risks (while considering options, costs vs. benefits, and consequences of failure).			
I am open to and seek out feedback.			
I am willing to join a group that collaborates and works together.			
I value and create change.			
I challenge bureaucracy and disempowering actions in all forms.			
I frequently act on things that others would consider risky.			
I routinely challenge status-quo thinking.			
I continuously seek ways to advance beyond today's thinking.			

FINANCIAL RISK

QUESTION	LOW	MED	HIGH
How important is financial security to me?			
How much financial risk am I willing to take?			

Source: Adapted from the work of Rita Bailey, consultant and CEO of Boxages, LLC.

REFLECTION:

How do you feel about your responses? Do they spur you to take more risk?
Less risk?

How might this information contribute to your personal vision?

STRENGTHS

In the programs I deliver, we often use the CliftonStrengths material. I won't try to replicate that body of work here. I encourage you to go online and complete the online assessment (StrengthsFinder) and determine your Top 5 strengths. There is considerable research that shows that the best leaders are authentic leaders that play to their strengths. And if we are able to use our strengths in 50 percent or more of our job responsibilities, we are happier, more productive, and more engaged. Each of us has aspects of our jobs that are not our favorite parts. Knowing I spend more than half of my time teaching and coaching gives me great joy.

Once you've received your Top 5 strengths, reflect on the following questions.

ACTIVITY:

Strength 1: _____

How do you use this strength in your current role?

What changes would you need to make to use it even more?

Strength 2: _____

How do you use this strength in your current role?

What changes would you need to make to use it even more?

---

continued

Strength 3: _____

How do you use this strength in your current role?

What changes would you need to make to use it even more?

Strength 4: _____

How do you use this strength in your current role?

What changes would you need to make to use it even more?

Strength 5: _____

How do you use this strength in your current role?

What changes would you need to make to use it even more?

And how can knowing your strengths contribute to your Personal Vision?

FEARLESS QUESTIONS

Fearlessness is not being afraid of who you are.

~ Chögyam Trungpa

The following questions are based on the work of Dr. Margaret Wheatley contained in her DVD titled *Eight Fearless Questions*. I offer four of these questions to you as a way to stretch your thinking as you develop your personal vision.

The first question asks us: "Does the world need us to be fearless?" If you agree with the definition of fearlessness in the Trungpa quote, I daresay the answer is, "Yes!" This is at the very heart of being authentic. Fearless and courageous people will rarely, if ever, be in the majority. You have to come up with your own answer to this question. As you look around, I would encourage you to notice whether new behaviors are called for on your part. What would that look like as part of your vision?

A second question is: "Can I bear witness to what is?" Bearing witness has two very different meanings. One is to look reality in the eye and practice the art of nondenial. When someone presents us with information that truly challenges our thoughts or feelings, do we push it away, deny it, or resist it? Or do we take it in and consider it thoughtfully?

A second definition is that we're willing to stand *with* people who are having a hard time, and we don't try to fix them or solve their problems for them. As a parent, teacher, coach, or anyone in a helping profession, this is *really* hard. This is about knowing that it is their work to do and no one else can do it for them, no matter how hard we try. Each of us has people or situations in our lives that we want to fix—an alcoholic parent, a child who doesn't study enough, an annoying coworker, and the list goes on and on. Is there something in your personal vision that would allow you to bear witness to a challenging situation and be okay with just standing with that person, seeing the situation for what it is and letting go of the need to "fix it"?

The third question is: "Can I work with what's available?" We all know there is never enough time in the day, we're always short-handed, and the budget is typically a constraint. I offer that each of us has enough to get started. Margaret Wheatley tells a beautiful story about working with what is and what is available in a story[2] about a concert delivered by Itzhak Perlman:

Itzhak Perlman is a world-renowned violinist, conductor, and music teacher. Perlman was stricken with polio as a child. He has braces on both legs and walks with the aid of crutches. In one of his concert performances, one of the strings on his violin broke. (Don't we all have those moments when something in our lives breaks or we have an unexpected event?)

He sat for a moment, closed his eyes, and then signaled the conductor to begin again. Rather than replace the string, he chose to play the remainder of the concert with only three strings. Any classical musician knows this is an extraordinary feat. The audience understood the effort it took to deliver a concert with only three strings and rewarded his efforts with cheering and thunderous applause.

When finished he wiped the sweat from his brow and stated, "You know, sometimes it is the artist's task to find out how much music you can still make with what you have left."

A powerful message. Re-read the last line—you are the artist of your life. How can you appreciate what is available to you right now and take that into consideration as you write your personal vision?

The last question is: "How do we imprison ourselves?" We're not locked away, though we may be locked up for a wide variety of reasons.

---

2   This article appeared in the *Houston Chronicle* newspaper as reviewed by Jack Riemer. As I was verifying all the references, there seems to be a question regarding the validity of this actually happening. I was crushed, because I was so moved by the story and the important message it conveys. I searched to see if there was another story as compelling. I couldn't find one. I hope you'll indulge me including this story as a representation of "still making music with what you have left."

In your personal vision, strip away those limits and allow yourself to think wide, think big.

As you think about these fearless questions, daring to be your most powerful self, I remind you of the Marianne Williamson prayer that includes the following lines: "Your playing small does not serve the world. There is nothing enlightened about shrinking so that other people won't feel insecure around you. We are all meant to shine . . . It's not just in some of us; it's in everyone. And as we let our own light shine, we unconsciously give other people permission to do the same. As we are liberated from our fear, our presence automatically liberates others."

ACTIVITY:

Does the world need me to be fearless?

Can I bear witness to what is?

Can I work with what's available?

How do I imprison myself?

How do I offer my work? As a gift? As needing to get something like approval?

WHAT IS A VISION?

A vision is the manner in which one sees or conceives something. A mental image produced by your imagination. If you were to fast-forward your life, what would you like to see? Robert Fritz describes "the anatomy of a vision" in his book *The Path of Least Resistance*. I have adapted and summarized some of his points in the following list, and I invite you to think about these elements as you envision your future.

Your Personal Vision:

- Is motivated by your own desire, without obligation or perceived need to achieve it. (You can dream big and not be limited by any perceived obstacles.)

- Stands on its own. It is not a reaction to other circumstances. (You don't need to do a competitive analysis to view others' personal visions; this one is yours and yours alone.)

- Answers the question, "What results do I want to create?" It focuses on results, not how to achieve the results. (This is about outcomes; it is not about an execution plan for achieving your vision.)

- Is affirmative, descriptive, and specific. (Write as much detail as you can, including the literal visual image: Where are you? Who is with you? Make sure you're smiling.)

- Is situated in the future, yet you can see yourself in it right now. (Think about and write about your future in the present tense.)

- Reflects your thinking when "the sky is the limit" and isn't constrained by what appears to be possible or doable. (Don't limit yourself. Don't "should" on yourself. Don't talk yourself out of it. You don't have to explain or justify it.)

- Arises from the moods of curiosity, passion, wonder, and aspiration. (I often think about myself as a five-year-old when I review this bullet. Remember how we wanted to be a teacher, a ballerina, and a grocery store checkout lady—yes, that's the kind of thinking we're encouraging.)

The following Creator-Reactor chart is adapted and formatted from Jim Collins's book *Good to Great: Why Some Companies Make the Leap and Others Don't.*

Creator	Reactor
Internally driven; externally aware	Externally driven; without intrinsic passion
Pursues creative strategy	Pursues competitive strategy
Discovers inherent talents and applies them	Agenda of competence set by the outside world
Many "once-in-a-lifetime" opportunities	Few "once-in-a-lifetime" opportunities
Ambitious first and foremost for the work	Ambitious first and foremost for self
Focuses on building relationships	Focuses on transactions
Values self-improvement for its own sake	Driven largely by comparison to others
Sets long-term goals	One year is long term
Core values inform all efforts	Nothing is sacred; expedience rules
Seeks self-actualization	Seeks success

And now you're ready. Consider your personal and professional values. Determine how much risk you're willing to take. Get clear about your strengths. Be fearless. Now find the right place for you to create your Personal Vision—a journal, a notepad, your laptop. Where you capture it is less important than just getting it out of you and down "on paper."

If you find yourself having trouble getting started, just start writing. There is an absolute connection from our brains to our hands. Even if you start writing, "I don't know what to write," or capture your questions or draw images, all of that can be the beginning. You'll be amazed at what you can create. If you get stuck, put it away and come back to it. Make every effort to write your Personal Vision before you review or explore others' personal visions. To be an authentic leader, your Personal Vision is your own. You can do this!

PART 1 DISCUSSION QUESTIONS

Some of you will be reading this book all on your own. Others may be reading and reviewing the book as a book club or women's group. At the end of each section, I've included some reflection questions that focus on what you've learned from the section and how you plan to apply it in your life.

If you are reading the book as a group, I encourage you to answer the questions individually before discussing them as a group. You want to do your own personal work. Once you hear others' responses, you can add, change, or even delete items in your own responses. Remember, women learn through stories. Share yours freely and deeply, and listen as others do the same.

SECTION REFLECTION QUESTIONS:

What did you learn about yourself while reading this section?

What stands out for you about power?

What three things will you do differently as a result of learning more about the differences between men and women (e.g., brain physiology, invisible differences, masculine/feminine attributes)?

How are you feeling about what you have read so far? What are three things you'll do differently going forward based on what you've learned?

PART 2

INTERPERSONAL RELATIONSHIPS

CHAPTER 4

WOMEN SUPPORTING WOMEN

There is a special place in hell for
women who don't help other women.

~ Madeleine Albright

"**H**ere's to women supporting women" has been one of my mantras
from the beginning of this journey. I will often use it as my email
sign-off when connecting women or making an ask for another woman.
It is not my intention to support women blindly. Instead, I am always
aware of alignment of values and intentions. I am also very cognizant
of wanting to "bust the myth" of women not supporting other women.
What breaks my heart is hearing women declare "too much estrogen in
here" as they enter a room full of women and also hearing women say
repeatedly that they would rather work with men than women.

Women often have complicated relationships with other women. We
have grown up with fairy tales of princesses, wicked stepmothers, and

stepsisters, and there is no shortage of "mean girl" stories, books, and movies. A woman I met over twenty years ago cited this phrase that she had heard and witnessed herself: "Men kill their weak; women kill their strong." Oh my—that phrase stopped me in my tracks!

We have a lot of work to do. I'm happy to say that I have seen this sentiment change considerably in the twenty years I've been doing this work. We are getting beyond the queen-bee syndrome, which is defined as a situation where high-ranking women in positions of authority treat the women who work below them more critically than their male counterparts. We're recognizing that one woman's success makes it easier for other women's successes.

Another aspect of women supporting women is having and maintaining a network of women supporters. There are many different roles that other people can play to provide support. To review a woman's reality, I will share this familiar story. When I was young, I had a lot of girlfriends, some closer than others. I almost always had a best friend or two that I could talk to about anything and that I could trust with my secrets. Even after school when I went to work, I still got together with my girlfriends for lunch, shopping, a movie, or happy hour. Then . . . I got married. My career was advancing and I spent more time at work. Then I had children. If I had any "free" time, I wanted to spend it with my family. So the first person to come off my to-do list was me, and then it was my girlfriends.

Admittedly, I have seen a few women in my programs who maintained strong connections with girlfriends or close female family members, but they were definitely in the minority.

Does this sound familiar? If so, let's do an exercise.

A STRONG SUPPORT SYSTEM

The following elements are needed if our support system is to be effective and cover all the bases.

CLARIFYING

Maybe you have one perspective on something and you would like another point of view. The people you are surrounded by have varying knowledge and experiences. They can help your fuzziness become clearer, give you a deeper or broader perspective, and may even ask you questions to clarify your own thinking. Think of examples in your personal life: "Should we move to ensure our kids are in a good school system?" "Should I continue seeing my current significant other, even though we've been on a rocky path?" And also in your professional life: "How should I handle a tough client situation?" "Should I apply for the promotional roles that will require me to do considerable travel?"

Enlist help from that person or those people you count on to help you see the challenge or the opportunity from all sides, people who help you consider the pros and cons and determine the tradeoffs inherent in most big decisions.

COMFORTING

Name those people you want to be with when you want to be comforted. Maybe you've had a really tough day or challenging week. You want someone to acknowledge how you're feeling and assure you everything will be okay. They have your best interest at heart. They don't say things like "suck it up" or "don't take it personally" or "it's not that bad." They respect that you're feeling exactly how you're feeling. Maybe they hold your hand or let you cry on their shoulder. Maybe they just listen. This person knows they are not there to fix it. Who are the people you count on for those comfort moments?

CONFRONTING

This is an interesting category. Often when one woman confronts another woman, things can go downhill quickly. And yet, we know we have situations where we need someone to challenge our think-ing, our assumptions, our interpretations, our self-talk, and even our intentions. The people we ask to support us by confronting us are likely to ask hard questions. They often hold up the mirror and help us to challenge ourselves.

They might ask us about what we are trying to accomplish. Is this about ego? About winning? About saving face? Are you in search for the best outcome for yourself, your team, your organization, your client, your student, your patient? Depending on your answer, they might ask you to play out the scenario so you can understand the ripple effect of your approach or decision. Confronting and challenging go hand in hand in this exercise. In addition to confronting your thoughts and ideas, these women may challenge your tone, your timing, or your body language. Who do you trust to challenge or confront you, knowing they are doing so with your best interests in mind?

CRISIS

You may like to think you can handle anything and everything that comes your way. You may even consider it a sign of weakness to ask for help, or convince yourself that everyone else is busy, too, so you can't really ask them. Yet we all know there are moments when we need a helping hand.

For example, you're out of town on a work trip and your child's school calls to say your son or daughter is running a fever and they need to be picked up and taken home. The school has been unable to reach your designated contact. Who do you call that you know will willingly and lovingly pick up your child and take great care of them until you can get home? Or maybe an important customer is demanding to speak to "someone in charge." Normally, that would be you; however, you are about to walk into a meeting where your participation is required. Who do you call that you know will handle the unhappy customer appropri-ately, making the right commitments and following through?

CELEBRATING

On the surface, this one might seem easy. It's a fun time; it's a celebration. Something amazing has happened and you want that special someone to share it with. And yet, I have frequently heard stories that make this category no easier than the other four. Women are not so comfortable tooting their own horns. We worry that others might think us arrogant or pompous. We might even have doubts about whether or not we even deserve whatever recognition is being given to us. In other words, we may be our own worst enemy in celebrating our own achievements.

And let's face it, some people might be jealous or resentful that you're being celebrated. Perhaps they also applied for that promotional role. Or perhaps their child didn't make the varsity sports team. The names you list in this category are truly the people who are all in to celebrate the moment with you. They are as happy for you as they would be for themselves. You don't have to worry that they might try to rain on your parade, downplay your accomplishments, or make sarcastic comments about ease or luck regarding your accomplishments.

In the following activity, I have included categories of support for you to consider. This is often a real eye-opener for women.

ACTIVITY:

In the following table, list the women (or men if you don't have women you can legitimately list) in your personal and professional network—people you can go to when you need support in one of the five listed areas.

	Personal	Professional
Clarifying		
Comforting		
Confronting		
Crisis		
Celebrating		

REFLECTION:

Was the same name in every box?

Did that name belong to your spouse, partner, significant other, parent, or sibling?

Was it hard to think of names?

My experience in doing this exercise hundreds of times is that the answer to each of these questions is yes, yes, and yes. It is often a rude awakening or an "aha moment" when you move through this exercise. So let's talk about developing and maintaining an effective support system.

DEVELOPING AND USING A PERSONAL SUPPORT SYSTEM

One method of acquiring, maintaining, and demonstrating one's interpersonal competence is to have a network of supportive relationships that can be drawn on as needed to help you achieve your objectives. A well-developed support system includes a variety of types of individuals and is not limited to people who are, say, close or good at listening or giving advice.

It is a skill to be able to establish, maintain, and effectively utilize a support system. As with all relationships, support systems can be difficult to establish, counterproductive, disappointing at times, and somewhat unpredictable. They take energy to maintain, and can also be used as crutches that make an individual more dependent rather than more resourceful.

Keeping your support system up-to-date and relevant to your goals requires ongoing assessment of the kinds of people who are currently available, letting go of those who are not relevant or who in fact are sabotaging your efforts, and building in new people who could be of assistance.

Supportive people may or may not be aware that they are a part of your system, and they may or may not be aware of the other people who are important in your life. The relationship may be close and personal or quite distant and impersonal. But it is important that they be useful and that the relationship be equitable and fair.

It is not necessary that support systems be reciprocal. However, most of us do function as parts of other people's support systems. It is an equally important skill to know how to *provide* support in a variety of ways. Analyzing how one becomes part of another's support system and how one leaves that support relationship can provide a basis for increasing your own interpersonal competence.

DEFINITION OF A SUPPORT SYSTEM

The definition given below is broken into phrases for the purpose of elaborating on some of the major issues involved in building an effective support system.

A support system is:

- a resource pool

- drawn on selectively

- to support you

- helpful in moving in a direction of your choice

- a relationship that leaves you stronger

The resource pool consists of people, things, environments, and beliefs. However, primary emphasis will be given to the issues concerning people and relationships. It is important for us to be *aware* of those individuals who could *potentially* be a part of our support system. This requires some skills at scanning your world and keeping an open mind about the possibility that any given person may be a relevant resource. It is helpful to be proactive in reaching out to locate and identify people, since the appropriate people are unlikely to come to you. The size of the resource pool is important; larger and more complicated systems require a lot of energy to sustain, while small systems may not have the range of resources that you need. The composition or variety of people thus becomes an important criterion in building an effective system.

Drawing on people selectively requires skills in choosing appropriate people and keeping those people who are not particularly helpful from getting in the way. It involves taking the risk of asking for support and being rejected or let down. It may also occasionally require dealing with jealousy and competition among those people in the system who would like to be asked for assistance and feel left out when you call on someone else. Willingness and availability are also obvious requirements for those people we ask for support.

Asking others *to support us* is often difficult. It may, for example, arouse feelings of guilt—we may think we're "imposing." Asking may feel like an expression of weakness or an admission of failure. It also opens up the fear that we may become dependent on another person rather than being self-sufficient. We do need to be open to help from others, willing to make demands on other people, and clear about the expectations we have of them.

To move in a direction of your choice requires you to be able to distinguish your goals from those of other people and organizations. Then you can move toward achieving *clarity* so you are in a position to make a *declaration* of that direction that can be understood by others. It means making a commitment, even if only for a short time or somewhat tentatively.

Ideally, a good support system will *leave you stronger*. It confronts you with your own ambivalence about growth and often will generate new demands as others perceive your strengths. If, based on the support you've received, you are now clearer and can act with more confidence, you may not have to rely on others. For example, you won't need to have them review your slide deck presentation to the board. Your self-assurance may negatively impact those relationships.

FUNCTIONS OF SUPPORT SYSTEMS

Support systems can be used for several different purposes, depending on the situation confronting an individual:

- **Reestablishing Competence**: Particularly in times of high stress or major transitions, you may find yourself functioning at a low level of competence. This may be because of anxiety, the energy it takes to cope with a crisis, physical and emotional difficulties, or overload of demands on you by other people. A good support system can help you cope and return to your previous level of functioning.

- **Maintaining High Performance**: It can be equally important to have access to resourceful people when you are doing well in order to maintain that level of activity. Although it may be easier to use assistance when performing at a high level, many people tend to neglect their support systems at such times, finding it more difficult to ask for help when they need it.

- **Gaining New Competencies**: A somewhat different function of support systems is to assist in developing new skills. What is needed here are people who can challenge, serve as teachers and models, and provide emotional support during periods when you may be feeling awkward or inept in dealing with new situations or new roles.

- **Achieving Specific Objectives**: Many of the objectives we strive for cannot be met without collaboration with and contributions from a number of people. This often requires people who have skills and resources that you do not have or that you do not wish to develop.

These functions of support systems are focused primarily on the individual. They often can help an individual contribute to organization goals and objectives, but it is equally important that support systems be used when individuals find themselves in conflict or opposition to the directions of other people, groups, or organizations.

Support systems are particularly helpful in coping with the stress that accompanies transitions in relationships, roles and positions, or careers. Skills in establishing new support systems are essential for successful transitions into new environments. You may find yourself in situations where you need support to live out the espoused values and principles of your organization. Ensuring customers are satisfied and treating all employees with dignity and respect requires constant heavy lifting. In other situations you may need support to challenge directives or decisions that you perceive are contrary to "doing the right thing." Examples are allowing someone to work from home more frequently to provide care for an aging parent or giving someone extra time off beyond the policy because the employee has put in so many extra hours to achieve a particular outcome.

DIFFERENT TYPES OF SUPPORT-SYSTEM MEMBERS

Support-system members can function in a number of different ways. Some people fill a variety of roles, while others may offer only a single type of support. The following list illustrates some of the different functions of support-system members:

- **Role Models** – people who can help define goals for positions you might assume in the future. Role models not only show what is possible but also are a source of valuable information about the opportunities and problems associated with a given role.

- **Common Interests** – people who share common interests or concerns and are especially important in keeping you motivated, and in sorting out problems that are primarily those of the individual from problems imposed by the larger system and that require collective activity to bring about change in that system.

- **Close Friends** – people who help provide nurturance and caring, and who keep you from becoming isolated and alienated.

- **Helpers** – people who can be depended upon in a crisis to provide assistance. These people are often experts in solving particular kinds of problems and may not be the type with whom you would choose to have a close or personal relationship.

- **Respect Competence** – individuals who respect the skills you have already developed and who value the contributions that you make. They are particularly helpful during times of transition when you may be feeling unsure of yourself in developing new skills.

- **Referral Agents** – people who can connect you with resources through their knowledge of people and organizations, where you can further obtain needed assistance.

- **Challengers** – people who can help motivate you to explore new ways of doing things, develop new skills, and work toward the development of latent capabilities. They often are people who you may not care for as personal friends but who are useful in your development.

SOME PRINCIPLES IN USING SUPPORT SYSTEMS

- **Parsimony** – An attempt should be made to keep the system as simple as possible to minimize the energy it takes to maintain it.

- **Maintenance** – It is wise to keep relationships current and up-to-date so that when you do need to draw on people, they are informed and appreciative of your need for their assistance.

- **Equity** – The relationship should be one in which both sides feel that there is a fair arrangement, whether it be accomplished by returning help, payment of money, joint sense of accomplishment, or whatever else makes sense. Guilt can easily build up when there is a sense of indebtedness that cannot be repaid.

- **External Support Base** – The primary base of support for being competent should be external to the system in which you are using your skills. Leaning on people inside the system in which you are trying to be competent often leads to a sense of dependency. (Paradoxically, when you are seen as having an external support group, people inside the system are also more likely to be supportive.)

- **Backup Resources** – It is wise to have several places you can turn for particular kinds of support to reduce the sense of vulnerability you feel in case an individual is unavailable or unwilling to help in a given circumstance.

- **Feedback** – It is important that feedback be given both ways to check on how each person feels about the process of giving or receiving assistance. Helping often creates resistance and/or resentment. Unless there is a means of keeping track of the process, the relationship is likely to erode over time.

ASSESSING YOUR SUPPORT SYSTEM

Now that we have gained some insights regarding support systems, let's assess yours. As you reflect on the names you included in each category, ask yourself the following questions.

- **Mix**: Are they like you/different from you—gender, age, race, etc.?

- **Repetition**: Do you find the same people in several of the boxes?

- **Roles**: Are individuals in traditional roles? Are you limiting your options in that regard? Maybe some reorganizing of who supports you in which category would benefit you.

- **Number**: Women in your support system—too few, too many, right number for you?

- **Geography**: Are people in your support system close by, in terms of physical proximity, or far away? Sometimes proximity maximizes the benefit of having an individual support you. Are you considering all possibilities when "recruiting" support-system members?

Do you have the mix you need and want? If not, what can you do to change that? Every person may not be effective in being a support person in all five categories. Different people have different experience and expertise in these categories. Make sure you are not relying on one person to fit all needs. Expand your network to include people who are skilled and valuable in each of the specific categories.

KEY IDEAS

Here are a few thoughts to focus on as you build and sustain your support system.

- Let people know they are an important part of your support system. Thank them for their support, situationally and collectively. Most people I know consider it an honor and a privilege to be considered and take this responsibility seriously.

- Keep the system simple. It should increase your energy, not drain it.

- Maintain the system. Keep in touch with people so they are ready when you need them. Don't just contact people when you need something. Develop and maintain a strong overall relationship.

- Keep the relationship equitable; give and take without indebtedness.

- Develop backup resources in case someone isn't available when you need them.

- Invite feedback, and likewise, tell the helper how they are doing.

REFLECTION:

What changes do you want to make to your support system?

Who do you need to tell that they are part of your support system?

How will you thank those people who have been a part of your support system?

MISOGYNY

Rita J. Andrews, a dear friend and colleague, was a longtime facilitator in our Power of Self Program. She wrote, spoke, and taught eloquently and competently on the subject of misogyny. In the early years of our program, many women didn't know what the word meant. Merriam-Webster defines misogyny as "hatred of, aversion to, or prejudice against women." If they did know what misogyny was, they often connected it to domestic abuse or sexual assault.

The word and the topic have become more mainstream—sadly because it is alive and well in our world today, and thankfully, it is now being exposed so that we can work to fight misogyny on every level. What I want to do in this section is help you better understand misogyny, particularly as it relates to internalized misogyny and how women can display misogynistic behaviors toward other women.

The following passage is my adaptation of an excerpt from an article by Rita.[3]

WOMEN AND INTERNALIZED MISOGYNY

Although the subject of misogyny isn't often discussed—either in mixed company or in all-female groups—the impact of misogyny is felt in every society and organization throughout the world. When misogyny *is* discussed here in the United States, the focus is often on our country's patriarchal legacy.

In women's groups, for example, we talk about how men have historically been accorded power, privilege, and access, while women have not. As a facilitator who speaks of misogyny often, I have cautioned participants that, while I believe the power differential between men and women is an excellent place to start, I am particularly concerned with women's own internalized misogyny.

As women, we have to become more aware of what we do to ourselves and other women. If we ignore it, this phenomenon will continue to influence every aspect of our lives. To shift the status quo and address issues of internalized misogyny, we must first be able to see it.

---

3   Rita Andrews (1944–2010) was an amazing colleague and supporter of women. She dedicated her adult life to supporting women, especially on tough topics. The material in this section on misogyny is based on Rita's research and teaching.

Here are ways that this dynamic shows up:

- **Questioning, Doubting, and Negating Oneself** – Women often begin their statements with the following caveat: "I'm not sure of this . . ." or "This is probably not true . . ." rather than making clear, direct statements (disclaimers). This is a very public way of questioning, doubting, and negating oneself. Often in all-female groups and mixed groups, participants will display this dynamic, completely unconscious that they're doing it. Highlighting and raising awareness of this behavior will help it to shift. It seems women are also willing to negate their contributions to organizational/team effectiveness. When complimented about a work contribution, some women will still reply, "Oh, it was nothing," rather than accepting the compliment.

- **Finding Oneself Unacceptable** – Our society constantly tells women they are physically unacceptable because they don't measure up to advertisers' images of beauty. This is particularly true for women of color, older women, and women who are considered overweight. It's also important to note that the idealized woman is air-brushed, filtered, and unreal. In addition to a narrow beauty standard, there are other ways women learn that who they are is unacceptable. In general, in our society, masculine qualities are often valued and feminine qualities are often consistently devalued. When I was starting my career, there were many subtle and not so subtle signals that "acting like a man" was preferred. Many companies had dress codes and many women's suits were fashioned after men's suits—same fabric with a skirt instead of trousers. I was often told "it wasn't personal; strictly business." I was challenged to hide my feelings because feelings weren't appropriate in business.

  I laugh out loud as I write this because of the naiveté and ridiculousness of this statement. Women tried "doing it like a man" and it failed pretty miserably. We were often clumsy in our efforts, and it didn't feel very genuine. We were not behaving within the stereotypical image of a woman in the men's eyes. It was a lose-lose situation. This lived experience is all a part of my journey that led to writing this book. I want each and every one of us to be our best authentic selves rather than trying to act like or be anyone else.

Therein lies our power. Women in organizations learn quickly that to be accepted, they must be "male identified"—in short, the better way is to "do it like a man." Recent *Catalyst* research finds, "to facilitate their advancement, the majority of women develop a style with which male managers are 'comfortable.'" But that isn't good enough either. When women choose to "do it like a man," they are criticized. Women talk about being coached in their organizations to avoid being too aggressive, too assertive, or too demanding. For men in organizations, these characteristics would be entirely appropriate and often encouraged.

- **Hating, Mistrusting Other Women** – How often have you said or heard other women say, "I hate working for women. They are so difficult!" This is internalized misogyny. In her work on jealousy, envy, and rivalry in girls, Anne Litwin shows where this mistrust comes from and how it results in horizontal violence—women hurting one another. One of the biggest questions among women at the start of an all-female group is, "How can I trust these women?" Often, this lack of trust comes from women's experiences with being socialized not to trust women—a blatant misogynistic message—and from experiencing one another's internalized misogyny.

- **Undermining and Not Supporting Women** – While a mentor is someone who has knowledge and will share it with you, a sponsor is a person who has power and will use it for you. When it comes to this important distinction, the evidence is clear: Research shows that women tend to be overmentored and undersponsored. There is a difference between being a mentor and being a sponsor. A mentor willingly shares information that can help you navigate your organizational system or help you handle a new or challenging situation. A sponsor is a person who is willing to put their political capital on the line for your benefit. People's tendency to gravitate toward those who are like them, on salient dimensions such as gender, increases the likelihood that powerful men will sponsor and advocate for other men when leadership opportunities are available. The similarity principle—affecting all workplace relationships—is even stronger when it comes to sponsorships because the stakes are higher.

Sponsorship is a relationship in which senior, powerful people use their personal clout to talk up, advocate for, and place a more junior person in a key role. While a mentor's knowledge and experience will not be depleted if shared with someone else, the political capital a sponsor spends fighting for someone to get a key assignment can no longer be used on something else.[4]

4　Herminia Ibarra, "A Lack of Sponsorship Is Keeping Women from Advancing into Leadership," *Harvard Business Review*, August 19, 2019.

ACTIVITY:

And now, let's do a personal exercise. If we were together in a facilitated session, I would ask you to "stand if you ever. . ." Though we're not together, I invite you to actually stand if the statement reflects your own behavior. There is something very visceral about this physical act of standing, sitting, again and again. It's not meant to be a shaming exercise, rather to generate meaningful awareness of how we can unknowingly or unintentionally display misogynistic behaviors toward ourselves or another woman.

Stand if you ever. . .

1. Discounted or doubted yourself
2. Apologized before presenting your ideas in a group or meeting, such as saying, "I may be wrong," or "This is probably a stupid question"
3. Felt like an impostor/fraud when you got a promotion or opportunity
4. Looked in the mirror and really disliked what you saw
5. Tied your self-image to your appearance or clothes

Note that these thoughts and behaviors reflect internalized misogyny.

Stand if you ever. . .

1. Told a joke about women in mixed company
2. Laughed at a joke told by a man at the expense of women
3. Assumed a woman got promoted because of who she slept with
4. Assumed a woman got a job because of a quota
5. Talked about other women with men in order to be accepted as "one of the boys"
6. Said another woman was "too sensitive about gender issues"
7. Listened to gossip about another woman
8. Passed on gossip that you heard about another woman
9. Ever got upset with another woman and denied it when she asked
10. Said, "She's such a bitch"
11. Were more critical of women in leadership than of men
12. Talked about a woman behind her back and smiled to her face
13. Made fun of another woman's appearance behind her back
14. Said, "I hate working for women"
15. Said or thought, "You can't trust women"
16. Breached a confidence and told another woman's secret
17. (Add what you are willing to say that you may have done that has not been said)

Note: If you're asking how you can better support another woman, these statements provide guidance on what not to do. Source: Anne Litwin and others.

WHAT YOU CAN DO

A collaborative experience in a women's group gives women a sense of being supported by other women, which is often something they haven't experienced before. If you want to be a better supporter of women, and perhaps a role model as well, here are six keys to addressing internalized misogyny:

- Make a decision to address misogyny in yourself and others.

- Begin to open your eyes and see the misogyny around you.

- Raise awareness with information and statistics.

- Help women to know when they are being misogynistic; call them out on statements about women that are generalizations and stereotypes, such as, "Women are so _____ (bitchy, undependable, emotional, catty, etc.)."

- Ask other women to point out your own internalized misogyny, such as when you make similar statements, or when you make self-negating statements, such as, "I may be mistaken, but . . ."

- Be compassionate—not judgmental—in your observations of your own or another's unconscious misogyny; otherwise, it's just more of the same.

COURAGE OF CONVICTION

There is one last point I want to make. Women often ask me what they should do when others—men or women—make disparaging comments about a specific woman or women in general. I'd like to share my own experience and approach to this situation. I invite you to think about it as a choice continuum.

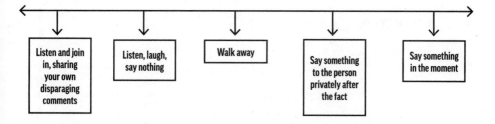

Admittedly, the older I got, the stronger the relationships I developed—along with gaining more positional power, I moved farther to the right on the continuum. I never added disparaging comments, though I can remember laughing nervously a few times. It is hard for me to admit that, even now. I feel ashamed to admit my shallowness and immaturity at that time. Over time, I became more courageous in asserting my convictions. In the spirit of offering a way to respectfully push back, I often asked privately, "Would you be okay if a group of people were talking that way about your wife, partner, daughter, or significant other?" I will add that people learned not to talk that way in front of me.

I am not naïve enough to think they suddenly stopped voicing their disparaging comments when I wasn't around. Several thanked me for "educating" them on how they were showing up. As we all know, we can't control what another person thinks, how they act, or what they say. What we *can* do is have the courage of our own convictions and stand up for our own values about treating others with dignity and respect.

REFLECTION:

How has your awareness and understanding of misogyny expanded?

What might you do differently going forward regarding your own behavior?

What opportunities do you have (or will create) to show support for another woman?

CHAPTER 5

BUILDING AND SUSTAINING TRUST

Trust is the foundation of effective relationships®.
Trust builds the bridge between the need
for results and the human need for connection®.

~ Dr. Dennis and Dr. Michelle Reina

"**T**rust" is a complicated word. I have heard many people declare that they absolutely do or absolutely don't trust someone. I have seen relationships built and developed on a strong foundation of trust. I have also seen relationships, both personal and professional, fall apart or be forever damaged because that precious trust was broken. I imagine you can say these same things in your own experience.

Before we go any further on this topic, I want to call something out. I looked long and hard for a quote about trust by a woman. The most frequent quote reference starts with "never trust a woman ..." It was a very disappointing experience. I then went to my trusted colleague Dr. Michelle Reina and asked her for an appropriate quote that encompasses the breadth and depth of trust. I invite you to think about the following questions.[5]

ACTIVITY:

How would you define trust?

What words come to mind when you hear the word "trust"?

What are your earliest memories of building trust in someone else?

5   Special thanks to Dennis and Michelle Reina for their longstanding commitment to helping all of us better understand trust and build stronger relationships as a result.

The definition of trust, according to Merriam-Webster, is "assured reliance on the character, ability, strength, or truth of someone or something." We all want trusting relationships. How do we get them?

UNDERSTANDING TRUST

There have been many studies about when and how babies and children develop, learn, or experience trust. Without diving deep into the research, let's just say it happens very early in life. When your baby can rely on you—can trust you—to meet their basic needs, they are building their capacity to trust another person. This is not at a cognitive level, as a baby's brain isn't that developed. Can a baby trust their caregiver to feed them when they are hungry, change them when they need changing, and cuddle with them when they need affection? Every time I say this in my classes and even as I write it now, a little shiver runs through me. As a twenty-six-year old giving birth to and caring for my son, I never even considered that. (And, of course, my mom-guilt hijacked my thinking.) Based on those early experiences, we then begin to see life through a certain lens. Of course, we have thousands and thousands of experiences that both reinforce and refute those experiences.

Now as adults, we are beyond basic care and feeding as the primary basis for our capacity to trust. As I've taught and learned from clients and participants in my programs, I've come to think about the adult framework for describing ourselves related to trust. Think about a visual of 0 to 100 on a vertical scale. Some of us start at 100 and trust almost everyone until they prove otherwise. We are all in. Oftentimes, there has to be a pattern of breaking trust for us to fundamentally not trust that person. Others of us start at 0 and trust almost no one until they have proven repeatedly that we can trust them. They have had to earn our trust. Those who start at 100 think about subtracting acts, language, or behavior. Those who start at 0 think about adding acts, language, and behavior. And there is one more facet to this contextual framework: there is a 40 to 60 midlevel that I call the "trust but verify" approach. I may extend a little or a lot of trust to another person and I will continuously be looking for behaviors that affirm the trust I've extended.

A couple of additional thoughts. First, *you have to give trust to get trust*. I had a woman in one of my classes who was a state-level judge. She declared to her classmates that they could trust her absolutely *and* that she would never trust any of them. And, guess what? Her classmates laughed aloud. The judge was surprised and taken aback by her classmates' reactions. As we paused to discuss what had just happened, this point of "you have to give trust to get trust" was playing out in real time. You can certainly imagine how a judge might be a bit skeptical about trusting others, given how many people stood before her courtroom declaring their innocence when they were, in fact, found guilty. An occupational hazard, if you will, impacting the judge's thoughts about trust. She learned in this classroom scenario that her professional experience and skepticism have likely served her well. However, in her personal relationships, they may have prevented her from having the kind of deep and significant relationships she wanted.

The second point is that *you are building, sustaining, or breaking trust in every interaction you have with another person.* These interactions can be a conversation, a phone call, a meeting, an email, a text, or even nonverbal signals such as a rolling of the eyes, avoiding eye contact, and the like. With this thought in mind, and knowing that trust is the foundation of every meaningful relationship, you want to be mindful as you write that email or formulate your response in a conversation. If you say or write something to another person, are you building, sustaining, or potentially breaking trust?

By now, you are likely beginning to see how complex the subject of trust is. You may be more curious about how to use what you've read thus far in this chapter. I am going to share what I consider to be the best framework and tools for increasing your ability to build and sustain trust in your relationships—both personally and professionally. Twenty-plus years ago, when I was searching for solid research and tools regarding trust, I found the book *Trust and Betrayal in the Workplace*, by Dr. Dennis Reina and Dr. Michelle Reina. I did some research and reached out to them to share my vision about a women's leadership program. I knew that I wanted to include the topic of trust because it is so foundational to relationships.

They responded enthusiastically and agreed to help me out. I spent long conversations with them in the early days and learned so much. Michelle even taught in my early programs. I felt I was learning from the masters. The frameworks are from their research and experience as well as my own over the past twenty-plus years focused on this important topic. If after reading this chapter you want to know more, I strongly encourage you to read their first book, as well as their subsequent book, *Rebuilding Trust in the Workplace*.

UNDERSTANDING WHAT BEHAVIORS BUILD TRUST

The following Reina-designed framework describes the behaviors that will enable us to build strong relationships.

The Reina Three Dimensions of Trust®

Trust of Capability®
Acknowledge abilities and skills
Allow people to make decisions
Involve others and seek their input
Help people learn skills

Trust of Character®
Manage expectations
Establish boundaries
Delegate appropriately
Encourage mutually serving intentions
Keep agreements
Be consistent

Trust of Communication®
Share information
Tell the truth
Admit mistakes
Give and receive constructive feedback
Maintain confidentiality
Speak with good purpose

reinatrustbuilding.com

TRUST OF CHARACTER®

I use a general definition of *Trust of Character*®: "I trust you to do what you say you're going to do when you say you're going to do it." In other words, I can trust your *character*. Now, let's talk about the specific behaviors that make up *Trust of Character*®.

Manage Expectations

When you look at the point at which relationship breakdowns occur, it often starts with your expectations not being met. Three kinds of expectations come into play here. The first are those you know you have and have expressed. The two of you have communicated and aligned your expectations, and you have walked through some examples to ensure each of you understands the other. The second is expectations that you know you have but have *not* communicated. If you've not communicated your expectations, it is impossible to get alignment and ensure understanding. And the third is expectations that you may not even know you have . . . until they are not met.

Expectations are about *how* we are going to interact, work together, or live together. Over the years, I've had my coaching clients and program participants develop their professional expectations and share them with me. I have consolidated the recurring expectations in the following list. It is a great starting point for you. Feel free to make changes to fit your individual situation.

EXPECTATIONS MENU

A. General Communications:

- Speak up when you are not clear or when you don't understand.
- Don't just bring me problems or ideas. Identify the business problem you're trying to solve. Ideally, bring options and their pros/cons along with your recommendation for the best option.
- If there are obstacles, tell me what they are, what you've done to overcome them, and what you need from me.
- Your time and energy, as well as your priorities, should always focus on creating value for our stakeholders.

B. One-on-One Meetings:

- Come prepared. Always have an agenda or a list of topics you want to discuss. Use the Check & Balance Template for consistent communication.
- Reach out in between meetings if you have questions or need direction.

C. Emails/Texts:

- Respond within 48 hours unless a shorter time is requested.
- Clearly state your "ask" if there is one. If you need me to do something, email is the most reliable way for me to remember. I keep my inbox small and use it as my to-do list.
- If I am copied on an email, please include me on your reply so I know you have responded and no further follow-up is needed.
- Provide context for a situation if you are asking for my advice, opinion, or a decision.
- I will send emails after hours and on weekends. That is my choice. It does not mean I expect you to respond at that time.
- Emails should be concise and laid out in a logical manner (what, so what, now what). Bullet points are preferred.
- I prefer a text if you need me urgently.

D. Meetings:

- State or know the objective of every meeting. Develop or ask for an agenda.
- Send agendas out at least twenty-four hours in advance.
- Be on time for meetings consistently. Respect everyone's time as well as your own.

continued

- End meetings at the scheduled time. Ensure objectives were met. Recap at end of meeting.
- Be present in and contribute to meetings. Provide comments and insights. Ask questions.

E. Project Management:

- Projects should be aligned with organizational and team strategies and priorities.
- If there are priority conflicts, discuss them with me.
- Make a work plan and walk through it with me at the start of projects.
- Set clear timelines and manage them. Tell me when you're going to miss a deadline. Don't tell me when it is due or wait for me to come ask you for it. This will allow us to reallocate staff and manage stakeholder expectations if changes are required. If a timeline needs to change, bring me your recommendations for moving forward.

F. Decision-Making & Escalations:

- You can make decisions based on your approved dollar level of $XXX. If something requires higher-level decision-making, bring me the business case for the expenditure. If applicable, include options and make a recommendation on which option you would choose.
- If a decision requires someone higher than me to approve, engage me early with an appropriate business case for the expenditure. If applicable, include options and make a recommendation on which option you would choose.
- If a stakeholder has concerns or questions, engage me as you deem appropriate. If it is something we have handled before, use your judgment. If it is a new issue or a highly visible client, come talk to me. Consider the risk involved. The higher the risk, the more I want to be involved. Keep me informed on all client concerns.

General:

- Ask for help.
- Be open to new ways of doing things.
- Work in a collaborative manner with all of our stakeholders.
- Deepen and expand your network for your benefit and for your team's benefit.

Expectations Menu

A couple of key points to consider in developing, communicating, and aligning expectations:

- Your expectations fit into the space of one page. Any more than that will be overwhelming for most people.

- Expectations are mutual. "Here are my expectations of you. They are reflected on page one." Page two is the other person's expectations of you.

- Start with defining expectations for your direct reports. Your team wants and needs that information from you.

- Developing, communicating, and aligning expectations is important in all of your relationships. Beyond your direct reports, go through the process with your boss, your peers, your customers, and the key stakeholders that you work with.

- If this is your first time developing and documenting your expectations, write them down and hold on to them for thirty days. During that thirty days, whenever you find yourself angry, disappointed, frustrated, or confused, it is likely related to an unmet expectation. Work hard to determine, understand, and define that expectation. Add it to your documented expectations list.

- Once you are comfortable with your expectations, share them with your team. Make sure they understand them by walking through examples. When you have worked through your expectations, turn the page over and develop and align their expectations of you. Examples might include giving timely constructive feedback, providing clear guidance and boundaries, being available for questions or challenges, or providing support for achieving their career goals.

- Share and review these expectations with every new person who joins your team. Make it a part of your onboarding process.

- Kick off every new year by reviewing these expectations. Perhaps you want to add, change, or delete some of your expectations. An annual review will reinforce your expectations and reduce the chance of breakdowns.

Now, let's think about personal expectations of family, friends, and loved ones. Maybe it's about domestic responsibilities with your family—making your lunch for work or school, checking homework, paying bills, or helping with grocery shopping.

What I often hear when it comes to personal and professional expectations is that so many of these expectations are "common sense." I smile when I hear this because my husband and I discussed (really, we argued) the topic of common sense. My view is that "common sense" was "common" when we all lived in the same small town, had the same teachers, neighbors, friends, ministers, were of the same generation and from a similar socioeconomic background, and shared similar life experiences.

That is not very "common" today. Children leave home to go to college, get their first job, relocate for a promotion, and travel more frequently for business or pleasure. For the most part, no matter where you grew up—whether it be rural or urban, or even a different country—you will be sure to encounter a wide variety of "common" sense.

Remember, others can't read your mind and may or may not share your "common sense" or life experiences. Developing, sharing, and aligning expectations is a huge first step in building and sustaining trust.

REFLECTION:

In what ways are your expectations being met by a key stakeholder group?

In what ways are your expectations not being met by a key stakeholder group?

What might be getting in the way of your expectations being met?

What can you do to better ensure your expectations are met?

Let's continue describing the specific behaviors that define *Trust of Character*®.

Establish Boundaries

I have dedicated an entire chapter to this particular behavior or act, as it relates to building trust with others; it is often how we betray ourselves. Anecdotally speaking, I find this to be a greater challenge for women than for men. Skip ahead to chapter 6 if you're ready to do a deep dive on this behavior.

Delegate Appropriately

I have included a tool in chapter 6 that helps you build this competency.

Encourage Mutually Serving Intentions

With whatever interaction you have with another person, each of you is committed to the success of the other. Make sure you are clear on what the other person is trying to achieve, and vice versa. One of the keys to success in displaying and living this behavior starts with you being clear about your own intentions, sharing those intentions, and ensuring you understand the other person's intentions. This is often referred to as "transparency of intentions." And before you can be transparent, you have to be clear from both a results and a relationship perspective.

Keep Agreements

This behavior gets to the heart of doing what you say you're going to do when you say you're going to do it. If you tell me you will get something done by Tuesday at two p.m., I can trust that it will happen. Now, let's be real. There will be times when any one of us is going to miss a deadline. Perhaps we're operating on overload or there was a last-minute surprise.

The key here goes back to managing expectations. My expectation of you is that you will let me know the minute you think you are going to miss a deadline so I can potentially help you get things back on track. I can reallocate resources. I can manage the customers' or stakeholders' expectations. It's much easier to handle missing agreements ahead of time rather than when they are due, or even worse, after we've missed an agreement or deadline.

Be Consistent

Another way of thinking about this is being predictable. Even if you don't like the way your boss makes decisions or handles difficult conversations, you can predict your boss's behavior and plan accordingly. Ask yourself how consistent you are. Are you always loud? Quiet? Are you always fast? Slow? Do you always speak first? Last?

I want to share my own aspiration for being consistent. I want others to be able to predict with great consistency that I will listen and be thoughtful in my response. This ties in very closely with one of my Foundational Elements, that the answer to every leadership question is, "It depends." Based on the situation, maybe I speak up or maybe I don't. Maybe I give an answer or maybe I ask a question. I want to be clear in my intentions and thoughtful in my responses. And you can predict that approach with great consistency and reliability.

TRUST OF COMMUNICATION®

My general definition of *Trust of Communication*® is: "I trust you to give me complete, accurate, and timely information. I trust you to fully disclose information." Here are the specific behaviors that reflect *Trust of Communication*®.

Share Information

You may have heard the adage that "knowledge is power." I always wanted to add "when shared." When you don't share information, you are preventing others from making a fully informed decision. It reminds me of the elementary child taunting and teasing another child with, "I know something you don't know." This often sends the message that you are "more than" the other person. And then there's that famous line from the movie *A Few Good Men*, when Jack Nicholson's character declares, "You can't handle the truth!"

To share information with another person reflects your trust in them to use the information to make the best decision, to broaden their perspectives, and to build their critical thinking skills. I remember my first account executive role. My company had acquired a company and I was asked to play a leadership role on this customer account. Our mandate was to reduce expenses and get the staff that came to us through the acquisition on board with my company's values and ways of doing business.

Computer-processing expenses were high and represented a large percentage of our overall operating expenses. I brought in all the leaders, including managers and supervisors, and shared the financial information with them. We brainstormed ways to reduce those expenses. However, when my leadership chain learned I had shared this information, they were concerned. Many of these leaders had been employees of our now customer only weeks before. What if they shared that sensitive financial information with their friends who were now our customers?

Thankfully, the story ends well. Because I had demonstrated my trust in those leaders, they used it for good. To my knowledge, they never shared it with their customer friends. They continued to come up with ways to reduce expenses and were more willing to share all kinds of information with me. Many told me that they never understood how their actions were driving up costs. The information I shared enabled them to make better decisions and increase their accountability for better results.

REFLECTION:

How is information treated in your organization?

What are your decision criteria for when to share or not share information?

Are there areas where you might be willing to share more information? How might you make that happen?

Tell the Truth

Often when I ask people to share initial thoughts about trust, the first word I hear is *honesty*. In fact, *Trust of Communication®* relies heavily on honesty. You expect others to tell you the truth—in a comprehensive, accurate, and timely way. Don't sugarcoat it or leave important things out. Don't make me come find you when I hear something from someone else that I would have wanted to hear from you. Have the courage and the integrity to tell your truth about the bad as well as the good.

You want others to trust you to do these things. The last thing any leader wants is to be making decisions that are ill informed.

I want to offer another consideration surrounding "truth." I emphasize, "Tell *your* truth." This may seem odd at first. Truth is truth. Right? The answer is, "Not exactly." You and I can witness exactly the same thing and come away with very different stories about it. How we share our truths says almost as much about ourselves as it does about what we each observe. Our life experiences, cognitive abilities, value systems, and perspectives influence our observations, interpretations, assumptions, conclusions, and actions. I recently heard a great quote by Jose Ortega y Gasset that I think speaks volumes: "Tell me to what you pay attention and I will tell you who you are."

Let me offer another tool for your tool kit. It is called the "Ladder of Inference" and was developed by Chris Argyris.

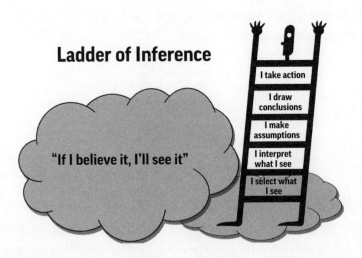

Ladder of Inference

"If I believe it, I'll see it"

I take action

I draw conclusions

I make assumptions

I interpret what I see

I select what I see

The Ladder of Inference included has been adapted from the work of Chris Argyris.

Let's start at the bottom of the ladder and proceed up each rung. You and I observe the same thing. Each of us **selects** certain facts about what each of us observed. There may be similarities and there will likely be differences. Once each of us has selected what we think are facts, we then make **interpretations** of those facts. Those facts can appear to us as good or bad, useful or not useful, smart or not smart, relevant or not relevant. We then make **assumptions** based on our interpretations, often about the person or people we are observing. We then draw **conclusions** and **act accordingly**.

And how long does it take us to go up this ladder? Nanoseconds. Our brains process quickly. Each of us has a ladder, and we're going up that ladder many times a day. Let me give an example that was shared in a program where I was teaching this tool.

> *Company A acquired Company B, which included a staff of about 300 people. Company A sent three senior executives to meet the entire staff at Company B and welcome them to Company A. What the Company B staff noted (facts selected) is that one of the Company A executives had slurred speech, was unsteady on his feet, and was in and out of the room a lot. They interpreted that the executive was drunk. They assumed this was considered acceptable and even appropriate executive behavior in Company A. They concluded they weren't sure that they wanted to work at Company A. They took action, and about half of the 300 Company B staff resigned over the next thirty days.*

Now, you might say the departure of Company B employees had nothing to do with the scenario described, so let me share a bit more information. I corroborated this story with one of the executives of the company where I was delivering this program, who also happened to be one of the three executives from Company A that went to welcome Company B staff to Company A. He followed up on the large exodus of Company B employees and was told repeatedly that many cited the "drunk executive" as the key criteria in their decision to leave.

MANAGING YOUR LADDER OF INFERENCE

Let me offer some coaching tips on how to manage your ladder.

- When you get to the top, ask yourself, "What else could be true?" You made up one story, and you can consider other possibilities as well.

- Then, share your own answers to these same questions. Where are there similarities? Where are there differences? I have done this exercise thousands of times since learning this tool thirty years ago and, wow, how it has changed my thinking, my approach, my decisions, and my relationships.

- Go back up the ladder together with your shared and expanded perspectives. You may decide you need to go through this process with other people involved in the situation. It may take a bit of time, *and* it will build trust with those you are involving. It improves your relationships and your decision-making. And your own learning will be enhanced.

The following is an "epilogue" to the example of Companies A and B, and in the spirit of "What else could be true?"—the executive had recently had a stroke, which is what prompted his physical behavior of slurred speech, unsteadiness on his feet, and going in and out of the room a lot. No one from Company B considered what else could be true or checked out their drunk-executive story. If someone from Company B had taken one of the executives aside, shared what they had noticed, and asked if there was anything they could do to help, they would have learned that he was recovering from a stroke and this was early in his reentry back into the workplace. The other two executives thought they were supporting the third executive by bringing him along for this welcoming group. They never considered that others would have very different stories. The executives were well-intended though not informed about our active ladders of inference.

These points, examples, and coaching tips are all in support of telling your truth as well as hearing the truths of others. You now have a way of getting below the surface of seemingly different, contradictory, or misaligned truths.

Admit Mistakes

To admit mistakes is, in fact, to admit one is human. None of us gets it all right all of the time. When you communicate that you've made a mistake, others feel they can trust you because you're not speaking only of your successes or rightness, nor are you blaming others for mistakes that you made. What prevents you from admitting your mistakes? How much risk is involved when you admit your mistakes? I often find that women are more likely to take ownership of mistakes, even when they didn't make them.

There are two "watch-outs" for women in this area. The first is our inclination to apologize. When I hear this and explore it further, it is often representing a sentiment that she is sorry something happened. I strongly encourage you to state specifically what you are sorry about. For example, "I'm sorry this happened to you" or "I'm sorry it didn't turn out the way you had hoped." The second "watch out" is taking responsibility for someone else's mistake in order to avoid uncomfortable conversations or unpleasant outcomes. Have courage to stay silent when you feel the urge to take responsibility for someone else's mistake.

For example, you are presenting material that someone else has researched and developed. Someone points out that something is an error or data is misrepresented. In this situation, state that you will look into it and get back to them. Then, encourage and coach the person to admit their mistake, take responsibility, and describe what they've learned or will do so the same mistake isn't made again. Now let me be clear, if you are in a leadership role and someone on your team makes a mistake, step up and take responsibility for the mistake. It *is* your responsibility to ensure you have appropriate checks and balances in place to ensure quality work is delivered.

By admitting your mistakes, you let people know you are a confident realist. People, including you, do and will make mistakes. And you are confident in your abilities and your willingness to put things in place so that similar mistakes don't keep happening. When you trust yourself enough to admit mistakes, you are a role model for others to do the same. Be intentional in how you respond when others admit making mistakes. Yelling, accusing, and blaming achieve nothing. Focus first on fixing the mistake. Focus second on what the other person learned from the mistake. Focus third on how the responsible person will ensure the mistake doesn't happen again.

If you are dealing with a large, complex, visible, lots-of-people-involved kind of mistake, this may require significant time, energy, and focus on your part. It will pay dividends in the long run because others will trust you to admit and own your mistakes and work hard to remedy the mistakes rather than blaming others.

Give and Receive Constructive Feedback

This is a major component of *Trust of Communication*® worth discussing at length. The bottom-line purpose of giving and receiving feedback is to help people learn, grow, and perform better. Always know *your* intention when giving feedback. Is it in a moment of frustration? Is it venting your own anger? Or is it because you believe your feedback can help the other person do better next time around?

Provide feedback when someone has done something really well. When that person receives your positive feedback, they are more likely to display those behaviors again in the future. I have a tool to offer that can support you giving constructive feedback. I've been using this 7-Step Feedback Model for decades—I developed it from experience and reading a lot about giving effective feedback.

7-Step Feedback Model

FEEDBACK FRAMEWORK

Step 1 – State the behavior as specifically as you can.

Step 2 – Describe the impact of such behavior. This could be impact on the budget, a contract, a customer or potential customer, a relationship, or even your views on being able to trust that person.

Step 3 – Describe your feelings and own them. For example, "I'm disappointed," rather than "You disappointed me." We choose how to feel (and respond) no matter what the circumstances.

Step 4 – Ask the individual to help you understand . . . and then listen. There are always two sides to every story. You will likely learn some new information. Be careful not to let them blame someone else. Don't discuss someone else's actions or behaviors. Your conversation is about the individual's specific behaviors (see step 1).

Step 5 – State what your expectations are going forward. (Remember the trust behavior of managing expectations in the *Trust of Character®* section.) If you haven't developed, shared, and aligned expectations with this person previously, now is the time. If you have communicated them previously, restate or reinforce your expectations. If there is a new or different expectation, share the expectation and get alignment around it.

Step 6 – Ensure they understand and agree to meet your expectation. This is a "look me in the eye and give me your word" moment. This is serious. You don't want a flippant, insincere, or begrudging agreement. Let them know you will hold them accountable for meeting your expectation. Accountability is a key ingredient, and there is no accountability without consequences. These are not hollow words from you. You have to be clear about what accountability and consequences you are thinking about. The best way to ensure understanding and alignment is to walk through a real example.

Step 7 – Determine whether the other person needs anything from you to ensure their success in meeting your expectation. Be careful not to take on too much, inevitably letting them off the hook for achieving the desired result. If it is a more junior or less experienced person, you may want more oversight, or it may require you to do a bit more reviewing and checking. If it is a more senior or experienced person, you may want to give them more autonomy.

Now let's walk through a conversational example so you can see how I would apply the preceding process, step by step. The following demonstrates for you how I would navigate a scenario where an expectation has not been met.

- **Step 1** – You have missed your last three project deliverable deadlines. Project A was due on October 1st and you delivered it on October 5th with no communication with me that it was going to be late. Project B was due November 3rd and I had to ask you about it on November 4th. Project C was due December 8th and I still don't know when it will be completed.

- **Step 2** – The impact of these missed deadlines is significant. The customer is unhappy with us and is about to trigger the penalty clause in our contract for missed deadlines. These financial penalties are serious and will be reviewed by senior leaders. We have had to work your team members overtime in order to keep subsequent deadlines from also being missed. My trust as well as the trust of your peers has been negatively impacted, given your track record of missed deadlines.

- **Step 3** – I am frustrated and disappointed in this pattern of you missing deadlines. Each time we've discussed this, you have told me it won't happen again and then it does.

- **Step 4** – Help me understand what is going on with all these missed deadlines. (The other person gives you their side of the story. Regardless of their explanation, the following steps will still be communicated.)

- **Step 5** – What I need from you going forward is to let me know the minute you think you might miss a deadline. Knowing ahead of time gives me more desirable and effective options. I can reallocate resources. I can remove potential or real obstacles you may be facing, and I can let the customer know what is going on so we can work things through.

- **Step 6** – Do you agree to let me know the minute you think you might miss a deadline? (Wait for their response.) You have two deadlines coming up. Is everything on track to hit those? (They might say, "No, I can't guarantee that I won't miss a deadline." Well of course they can't, and that is not your expectation. Your expectation is that they communicate with you in a timely fashion. That is totally within their control.)

- **Step 7** – Do you need anything from me to meet my expectations? (Then you would agree to—or not agree to—what the other person is asking from you.)

This model can be used for positive constructive feedback as well. Cite the effective or outstanding behaviors the person displayed. Perhaps your Step 5 expectation in this scenario is to keep up the good work or even teach and mentor others.

I recommend that, as you begin to use this tool, you write out your script word for word and practice in front of the mirror. When we hear the word feedback, we almost always assume negative feedback. You want the content, the specific words, and the tone to be effective in helping the other person improve or keep doing effective things. It is absolutely okay to bring your notes with you and to refer to them throughout the conversation. Let the other person know you have some notes and will be referring to them in order to cover everything. Knowing you have documented notes brings a seriousness to the conversation. If the feedback doesn't result in improvement, you now have documentation required for other potential performance management scenarios.

By *giving* constructive feedback, you are telling the other person, "I care about you, and you can trust me to provide feedback that will help you learn, grow, take on bigger responsibilities, and achieve career aspirations."

By *receiving* constructive feedback, you are telling the other person, "I trust and value your observations and desire to help me improve." Once you've heard the feedback, it is your choice as to what to do with it. If it is similar to feedback that you've received before, you may want to refocus your efforts. If it is new feedback and seems contradictory to other feedback you've received, you may want to check it out with someone you work with frequently or someone you know has your best interest at heart. Just because you may not like the person giving you the feedback doesn't mean you should ignore it. There may be some real value in what they are offering.

And one last point on feedback: It is my experience that the higher you go in the organization, the less feedback you receive. It is also my experience that women want feedback more frequently than men do—this is not good or bad, just different. If you keep asking for feedback, you may be perceived as needy, insecure, or lacking confidence. Let me offer a way to get the kind of feedback you want without ever using the word feedback. Here is an example.

> *Boss, we've just completed Big Project Alpha. It was a real learning experience and I'm proud of my team as well as my leadership. As I review this project, here is what I thought worked well (and then share your bullet points). Here is what I learned that will really help me going forward (and then share your bullet points). From your perspective, have I missed anything? You have led a lot of projects, and I would appreciate your insights (and then listen).*

Generally speaking, you are helping your boss to help you. It is much easier to fill in the blanks than it is to start with a blank sheet of paper. I encourage you to provide a follow-up email thanking them for their input (or stating your happiness that you hadn't missed anything) and incorporate their input if any was given. This communicates to your boss that you are a learner, confident, and self-sufficient, and gives you recognition for the good work you did. Be sincere. Be balanced. Be high level. Don't get caught in every detail or line-item task of the project. That can backfire. If your boss is smart, she'll file that email away and use it when she completes your performance review.

Maintain Confidentiality

This is a really straightforward behavior. You either trust someone to hold confidential information or you don't. When someone asks you if you can keep a secret, watch out. If someone starts the conversation with, "This is between you and me," watch out. If someone asks you if they can tell you something and says that you can't tell anyone, watch out. Never agree to hold something in confidence when you don't know what it is. Can you keep your commitment not to tell if you know it is putting someone, the organization, or the client at risk?

Coaching Tip 1 on this matter is to *never agree*—let them know that "it depends." Be direct and straightforward with the person wanting to share a secret with you. Coaching Tip 2 urges you to ask them if there is a reason they are sharing confidential information with you. Consider whether you need or want to know the information or not. Coaching Tip 3 is to challenge them on the issue of whether they should be sharing confidential information.

This isn't a shaming objective. It is about causing the other person to slow down and consider the unintended consequences of sharing confidential information. Depending on how well you know the person, you might remind them that they could be damaging a trusted relationship by sharing something told to them in confidence. If you demonstrate to everyone how you feel about confidential information—that you don't want to hear it and, therefore, you won't pass it along, you are demonstrating trustworthy behavior.

There will be times when you want and need to hear confidential information such as when someone is violating policies, violating ethics, or abusing staff. You can't step in to remedy such situations if you don't know about them. Let the person who is sharing the confidence with you know that if you deem it serious or egregious enough, you will have to act on it with the potential of sharing it with others. If you do these things, others will trust you. You are clear, direct, and intentional while also managing expectations and establishing boundaries.

And remember, every person you tell is likely to tell at least one other person, so don't be surprised when confidential information becomes hallway chatter.

Speak with Good Purpose

In basic terms, this behavior implies, "I can trust you not to gossip about me behind my back." Gossiping and sharing confidential information are at the top of the list of behaviors that break trust in most organizations. My one-line reminder on this behavior is "talk *to* me and not *about* me."

If you are unhappy with someone, talk to them about it. Someone else can't fix the problem you have with another person. It may be easier to talk about someone than it is to talk to someone. That doesn't make it right. Use the 7-Step Feedback Model as a framework for talking to the person. If someone tries to share gossip with you, let them know you don't want to participate in gossip. For some, that will be off-putting and they may not like your response. At the same time, they will know they can trust you not to be contributing to the rumor mill. Bottom line, I trust you more if you aren't gossiping about others. And if that is consistently true, you won't be spreading rumors and gossiping about me either.

TRUST OF CAPABILITY®

My general definition of *Trust of Capability*® is: "I trust that you have the knowledge, skills, and abilities to meet your agreements." I can trust your capabilities. And here are the specific behaviors that reflect *Trust of Capability*®.

Acknowledge People's Skills and Abilities

Much research in recent years has encouraged organizations to "play to people's strengths." Valuing others' skills and abilities builds trust and also shows confidence. You demonstrate your understanding and appreciation that we're not all good at everything. To pretend otherwise can be perceived as either naiveté or arrogance.

One of the things I've learned over the years is that even though someone works for or with you, it doesn't mean you know all their skills, abilities, and experiences. I encourage you to spend the time with your colleagues to understand their history. This may include functional knowledge and skills, industry or geography experience, or things they do in their free time. People may have board experience from their community or philanthropic engagements. Based on what you learn, you might assign them to a project that advances their career aspirations. Or perhaps you grant them greater decision-making authority, reflecting your trust in their capabilities. And this leads us to the next specific behavior.

Allow People to Make Decisions

This behavior is directly tied to you trusting the other person's judgment. You have a higher probability of success if you know and trust their skills and abilities. I am a big proponent of giving others the responsibility as well as the authority to handle their jobs. It broadens your understanding of how your work and your decisions impact other parts of the business or organization. Your direct reports will often have a greater appreciation of all the variables that need to be taken into account. By allowing others to make decisions, you are developing trust with them.

Involve Others and Seek Their Input

A first step in involving others is to seek their input. Ask them what they would do to achieve an outcome, lead a project, respond to a client question, solve a problem, or build a relationship. I have learned so much from other people whose knowledge, skills, and abilities are different from mine. It has broadened my perspective tremendously. By involving others, you are telling that person you trust and value what they have to say or contribute.

Help People Learn Skills

This behavior can take several forms. One form is to help them build skills to better perform in their current role. By the other person improving their performance and expanding their skill set, they will likely get a better performance evaluation and all that may result from that, like increased compensation opportunities. Another form is to help them get opportunities to work on important or high-visibility projects, or to help them build skills that make them viable candidates for promotions or career advancement.

When you help them learn new skills, you open up more possibilities for them. This tells them you trust their competence enough to invest the time and energy to support their growth and development. (It is also tied to the previous segment on "Encourage Mutually Serving Intentions" under the "*Trust of Capability*®" subhead.) The other person trusts that you have their best interest at heart and want to help them be successful.

REFLECTION:

Whose skills and abilities do you need to acknowledge?

What decision authority can you grant to someone on your team?

How can you help your team or colleagues learn new skills?

Now that you better understand the trust model and the supporting behaviors, let's think about how it applies to you on a practical basis.

UNDERSTANDING WHAT BUILDS TRUST

ACTIVITY:

Think of someone (one professionally and one personally) with whom you have high trust. What behaviors do they display that build your trust? Place a check mark (✓) in that column. Where would you "score" yourself on these behaviors?

Behavior	High Trust	High Trust	High Trust
Trust of Character*	Personal	Professional	Me
Manage expectations			
Establish boundaries			
Delegate appropriately			
Encourage mutually serving intentions			
Keep agreements			
Be consistent			
Trust of Communication*			
Share information			
Tell your truth			
Admit mistakes			
Give and receive constructive feedback			
Maintain confidentiality			
Speak with good purpose			
Trust of Capability*			
Acknowledge people's skills and abilities			
Allow people to make decisions			
Involve others and seek their input			
Help people learn skills			

By completing this activity, you are getting clearer about how people behave in order to build high-trust relationships. It also can give you insights on your own behavior, and how it influences and impacts your high-trust relationships. You can explore possible action steps to take in the following reflection questions.

REFLECTION:

Which of these behaviors is particularly important to you?

Which of these behaviors is particularly challenging for you?

Which of these behaviors would you like to work on?

What support do you need to begin practicing trust-building behaviors?

I hope that you have a much deeper and better understanding of trust. By describing the sixteen behaviors to you, my hope is that you can begin to understand what actions you need to take to build and sustain trusting relationships. This is important because, rather than saying you trust or don't trust someone, you can be much more specific and isolate specific behaviors that lead to your trust or mistrust of another person.

You may not trust someone to manage expectations and yet trust them absolutely about sharing information and keeping agreements. If we said we couldn't trust a person because they negatively displayed, compromised, or violated one of these behaviors, we wouldn't trust anyone. I don't know about you, but that doesn't describe the kinds of relationships I want to have. Rather than applying a broad-brush generalized type of distrust, it's important you specify which behavior is eroding your trust. If you think about someone you don't trust, which of these behaviors is absent or falling short?

Then you can use the 7-Step Feedback Model to share your thoughts. And that's a perfect segue to the next big trust topic: Betrayal.

UNDERSTANDING BETRAYAL

Betrayal is a big word and, dare I say, a scary word. We usually use this word when our trust with another person has been breached significantly and even heart-wrenchingly. I'm going to use three phrases interchangeably throughout this section: **betrayal**, **breach of trust**, and **breaking trust**.

Merriam-Webster's definition of betrayal is "violation of a person's trust or confidence, of a moral standard." The synonyms for betrayal include: back-stabbing, disloyalty, double-crossing, faithlessness, falseness, infidelity, treason, and two-timing, just to name a few. Even as I write these words, I shudder. I feel heavy just thinking about it. That said, not all betrayals are created equal. Let's do a little activity to help you think about breaches of trust in your life.

UNDERSTANDING WHAT BEHAVIORS BREAK TRUST

ACTIVITY:

Think of a time when you felt that trust was broken with another person—this can be a personal or professional experience.

What caused trust to be broken?

What is/was your relationship to the person who broke your trust (e.g., peer, boss, sister)?

How important was your relationship to that person at that time?

What specific behaviors broke your trust?

As you ponder your responses, what did you notice? How were you feeling in your body? Was it easy or hard to think of an example? I have had participants in my programs state that they don't think they have ever been betrayed. I have several reactions when I hear that statement. Lucky you! Are you sure? Quite honestly, if this is the case, then you're not paying attention. Sometimes things are so painful, we just try to push them away or minimize them. If they are too big, we can just feel overwhelmed. I am not here to judge how you've responded to betrayal. I'm here to help you better understand betrayal. And that leads us to our next tool and activity.[6]

Betrayal Continuum®

THE BETRAYAL CONTINUUM

MINOR (EXAMPLES)		MAJOR (EXAMPLES)	
UNINTENTIONAL	**INTENTIONAL**	**UNINTENTIONAL**	**INTENTIONAL**
Repeatedly arriving late for work	Gossiping, backbiting	Restructuring resulting in layoffs	Disclosing proprietary information
Not keeping agreements	Accepting credit for another's work	Delegating without giving authority	Sabotaging data systems

---

6   Thanks again to the Reinas for this helpful chart on trust and betrayal.

ACTIVITY:

Transfer the behaviors from the previous activity from the question, "What specific behaviors broke your trust?" (You might notice that many of these behaviors are the opposites of the trust-building behaviors from the previously discussed trust model.)

Categorize these behaviors into Minor or Major. This categorization is very personal to you. I can't give you an absolute definition. What is major to one person is minor to another, and vice versa.

◄─────── The Betrayal Continuum® ───────►			
Minor		Major	
Unintentional	Intentional	Unintentional	Intentional

Source: Trust and Betrayal in the Workplace®, 3rd edition

The Betrayal Continuum® is another tool in your tool kit. As you review your responses, what do you notice? Is everything in one category? What criteria did you use to determine whether something belongs in the "major" or "minor" category? If you chose a betrayal from a distant past, would you have categorized similarly then as you have now? In other words, has time changed your perspective? How does your relationship with this person who betrayed you impact how you categorize behaviors on the Betrayal Continuum®? My anecdotal experience is that the closer you feel to the person who betrayed you, the bigger the hurt or the more "major" it feels.

The Betrayal Continuum® is a useful tool when you're trying to sort out and analyze your thoughts and feelings. It is an opportunity to gain perspective. What may have seemed so major at one time may now seem minor to you. So, the next time you find yourself in a heightened state of anxiety regarding a breach of your trust, keep in mind that you've been there before and have come through it. A second way to use this tool is getting clear about the actual behaviors that broke trust, and providing feedback to that person using the 7-Step Feedback Model. This is particularly important if that person will continue to be a part of your personal or professional life.

A couple of other things to consider when using this Betrayal Continuum® tool. First, betrayal is in the eyes of the betrayed. You really can't know if it was intentional or unintentional. And yet, I imagine you are holding it as one or the other. That is another reason you want to have a conversation using the 7-Step Feedback Model. In step 4, the "help me understand" step, you may gain greater insight into the other person's intentions. What I personally learned around this consideration is about language. You can't tell someone you didn't betray them. That's not your call to make. What you can say is, "It was never my intention to betray you."

A second consideration is "beware betrayal buildup." Remember, "a dot is a dot, two dots are a line, and three dots are a trend." When someone breaks your trust in a minor, unintentional way, you want to provide feedback to them, restating your expectations going forward. If the other person continues with the trust-breaking behavior, you are now seeing a trend line. What was once a minor, unintentional breach of trust is becoming a major, intentional breach of trust. My coaching tip here is to address it before it gets to be a trend line and major betrayal. Handling it early is much easier than letting it build up. If you let betrayal accumulate, the stakes are higher and the relationship is at greater risk.

REFLECTION:

How often does betrayal show up in your life, both personally and professionally?

Are there themes of betrayal with specific people? Your boss, parents, or perhaps a certain friend?

What can you do to reduce future betrayals? Do you need to communicate and align expectations? Do you need to give feedback in order to let the other person understand the impact of their behavior on you?

What is something you need to do in the next thirty days to take actionable steps for current outstanding betrayal situations?

UNDERSTANDING HEALING FROM BETRAYAL

It is inevitable that trust will be broken in relationships throughout our lives. Our choice is how we will respond to it and whether or not we choose to rebuild a relationship based on trust. There is no shortage of material on the topic of building trust, but there is much less material on betrayal, and even less on rebuilding trust.

What becomes abundantly clear is that it is most difficult to rebuild trust without some form of forgiveness. Desmond Tutu wrote a book about healing from years of apartheid entitled *No Future Without Forgiveness*. Imagine the healing required during that historic time!

At Stanford University, Dr. Frederic Luskin heads a program called "The Forgiveness Project." What he is trying to teach us is key to rebuilding trust in the workplace and helping individuals to retain their power, decrease stress, and move forward. According to Dr. Luskin, few of us choose to forgive when people hurt us. Part of the problem seems to be that most of us don't know how to forgive. This is not something we learn in school. Dr. Luskin's research shows that "as people learn to forgive, they become more hopeful, optimistic and compassionate. As people learn to forgive, they become more forgiving in general." These enlightened individuals report significantly fewer symptoms of stress.

Dr. Luskin's 9 Steps to Forgiveness

1. Know exactly how you feel about what happened and be able to articulate what about the situation is not OK. Then, tell a couple of trusted people about your experience.

2. Make a commitment to yourself to feel better. Forgiveness is for you and no one else.

3. Forgiveness does not necessarily mean reconciling with the person who upset you or condoning the action. In forgiveness you seek the peace and understanding that come from blaming people less after they offend you and taking those offenses less personally.

4. Get the right perspective on what is happening. Recognize that your primary distress is coming from the hurt feelings, thoughts, and physical upset you are suffering now, not from what offended you or hurt you two minutes—or 10 years—ago.

5. At the moment you feel upset, practice stress management to soothe your body's fight or flight response.

6. Give up expecting things from your life or from other people that they do not choose to give you. Remind yourself that you can hope for health, love, friendship, and prosperity, and work hard to get them. However, these are "unenforceable rules": You will suffer when you demand that these things occur, since you do not have the power to make them happen.

7. Put your energy into looking for another way to get your positive goals met than through the experience that has hurt you.

8. Remember that a life well lived is your best revenge. Instead of focusing on your wounded feelings, and thereby giving power over you to the person who caused you pain, learn to look for the love, beauty, and kindness around you. Put more energy into appreciating what you have rather than attending to what you do not have.

9. Amend the way you look at your past so you remind yourself of your heroic choice to forgive.

Another one of my favorite quotes by Dave Willis: Holding a grudge doesn't make you strong; it makes you bitter. Forgiving doesn't make you weak; it sets you free.

The conversation on rebuilding trust comes full circle. Dr. Luskin's research focuses on forgiveness. The Reinas' research spans a broader set of considerations. I appreciate both perspectives. I lean to the Reinas' work, which they entitle Seven Steps for Healing. The significance of this approach in my mind is that I have to do my own work before I can think about having a conversation, much less about making a decision on whether or not I want to rebuild trust with another person. All seven of these steps for healing are totally within your control. You're not waiting on someone else to say or do something. Rather, you are doing your own work to get clearer about what happened, how you think and feel about it, and what you need to do so you can move on from it.

SEVEN STEPS FOR HEALING®

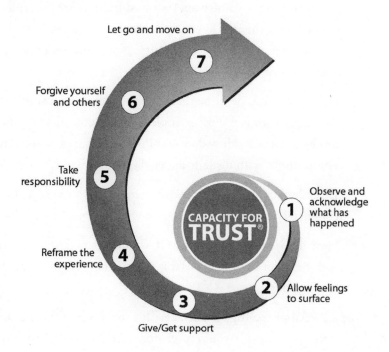

This model is another tool in your tool kit. Let's review it step by step. I encourage you to document your responses or thoughts around each of these steps.

- **Step 1 – Observe and acknowledge what has happened.** This sounds so obvious and yet we often don't know it is happening.

This is how we can get to that place of saying, "I don't think I've ever been betrayed." Here are some prompt considerations and questions:

- Describe what happened.

- Who betrayed you? What is the current status of your friends and family relationships and what was your relationship to them at the time of the betrayal? For example, was it your boss, your sister, your best friend? Are you still in contact with them? Do you still work for the same boss? Do you only see them at family events? Is that person no longer your best friend?

- How would you describe the nature of your relationship with that person today? For example, nonexistent, distant, cold, professional only. How do you think about that person today? For example, with disdain, anger, disappointment?

- Describe how you interact with them (e.g., cautiously, never, completely avoid them, etc.).

- How do you describe to yourself what happened between you and the other person? Does this differ from how you describe it to others?

- **Step 2 – Allow feelings to surface.** This step is easy for some and difficult for others. If you've ever done the Myers-Briggs Type Indicator, you know that some of us are Thinkers and others are Feelers. This particular dichotomy on that assessment reflects how we make decisions. It is the only one of the four dichotomies that is gender-biased, statistically speaking. About 60 percent of women are Feelers, though percentages may vary from country to country.

  In my programs, the Feelers can easily articulate their feelings; the Thinkers struggle. Early on, I found a list of Feeling words and have shared them with many program participants and coaching clients since. The Feelers thought it strange that others couldn't name their feelings. Many of the Thinkers found the list most useful, and one woman told me she carried it with her everywhere to help her get in touch with her feelings. A list of the Feeling words can be found in the appendix.

Regardless of how you get there, let your feelings surface. Maybe you're hurt, angry, or disappointed. Don't deny your feelings and don't listen to anyone who tells you, "You shouldn't feel that way." No one has the authority to tell you how to feel. And don't try to minimize or deny your feelings. When we suppress our feelings, they often show up anyway—and not in a healthy or useful way. I often say, "They come out ugly!" Once you've written down how you feel about the betrayal, how are you feeling now? Is there a sense of relief? Are you feeling vulnerable? Are you feeling lighter because you got it out of you and on paper? However you might be feeling, it takes us to step 3.

- **Step 3 – Give/get support.** Support can come in many forms. It may be talking with a friend, family member, mentor, coach, clergy, therapist, or trusted colleague. Maybe it's not talking at all. Maybe support means journaling about the situation. You don't have to go get a fancy or pretty new journal. The key is to get the feelings out of you and onto paper. Some of my program participants and coaching clients have shared that they capture the painful incident on their computers, pounding it out on the keyboard. Still others have used art therapy or cloud journaling as a way of expressing where they are and what they need. A key consideration is that you don't have to do it alone. It is not a sign of weakness to ask for help or support.

   When I'm in the throes of one of my own betrayal moments, *I am in it.* We can be narrow in our thinking, have blind spots, or be so emotionally invested that we can't be objective or consider other possibilities. ("What else could be true?" and the Ladder of Inference tool might be helpful.) Bottom line, feel your feelings and get support.

- **Step 4 – Reframe the experience.** This is where you can ask yourself, "What else could be true?" My personal reframing default is to ask myself, "What am I supposed to learn from this?" With support, try to pull yourself out of the emotional state of anger, hurt, or disappointment and think about how the betrayal is a wake-up call, conveying a message you needed to hear. Don't get me wrong—this is hard work! Being objective when you are hurting requires a lot from you, and that's why getting support is so important. If the betrayal represents a pattern in your life, determine what that pattern is. Maybe that is how you reframe the betrayal. You recognize it as a pattern and can now be on the lookout for it happening. And this takes us to the next step.

- **Step 5 – Take responsibility.** If getting betrayed is a pattern, you may need to examine how your actions and behaviors may be contributing to it. This is an example of you doing your own work.

  What part might you have played in contributing to the betrayal? I know I felt very defensive when I first asked myself this question when I was first introduced to this framework some twenty years ago. Two phrases also come to mind: "It takes two to tango" and "There are always two sides to every story." Maybe it's not what you did, but rather what you didn't do. Did you not communicate and get alignment on expectations? Did you not set and maintain boundaries? Did you not provide constructive feedback when your expectations were not being met and your boundaries not honored? Be careful not to stay in a defensive position. I often say it's okay to go there, but it's not useful to live there.

Also be careful not to make the other person wrong so that you can be right. This isn't about competition. It's about relationships and good mental health. Try to evaluate the situation honestly. What could you have done differently? What actions do you need to take now to work through the situation?

Disclaimer: I want to make an important point regarding this particular step. As you might imagine, I have heard many stories from women who were abused by husbands, fathers, brothers, or boyfriends. Or maybe they were sexually molested. These stories often surface when we're doing the Seven Steps for Healing work. I, in no way, am implying that these girls or women were in any way responsible for their experiences of abuse or molestation. Part of the abuse cycle is to blame the victim. It starts with the abuser and follows though to our legal systems. Rest assured, I hope and want for you to get the help and support you need to break the cycle.

- **Step 6 – Forgive yourself and others.** And we're back to forgiveness. First and foremost, forgiveness is for you. One of my favorite quotes on this topic is from Jonathan Lockwood Huie, an author who has been called "the philosopher of happiness": "Forgive others, not because they deserve forgiveness, but because you deserve peace."

  There are two considerations to think about: 1) forgiving others and 2) forgiving yourself. I always ask my program participants which is harder for them, and they have almost always said forgiving themselves. I have also found that the person who has betrayed you may never even know you feel betrayed, or to what extent. They are walking around oblivious to your thoughts and feelings. And you are the one carrying around the heavy load of betrayal.

  Let me share a story of what happened in one of my programs that ties trust, betrayal, and forgiveness together.

We were doing an exercise where program participants were documenting their various betrayals on a simulated Betrayal Continuum® posted on the wall. One thing that stood out was that over 70 percent of the women had been cheated on by their spouses or significant others. When we were discussing it as a large group, women shared that their response to such a betrayal was everything from "I've sworn off all men because you can't trust any of them" to "I didn't date for five years after I was divorced" to "I withhold my feelings because I don't want to be hurt again." We then broke into smaller groups to discuss it at a deeper level. Coming out of those smaller group discussions, many of the women discovered that it wasn't that they couldn't trust men. When they really dug deeper, they declared that they didn't trust themselves to choose a partner who wouldn't cheat on them. I have to tell you, I didn't see that one coming. As you might imagine, we spent considerable time diving even deeper and seeing parallels in other parts of our lives.

The ties I see here are that we extend trust to another person, they betray us, and we find it hard or impossible to forgive them. We carry that bitter feeling of betrayal around with us for a long time, and then we discover that the first step is to forgive ourselves.

Can you relate to this story? Can you think of an example where forgiving yourself would be appropriate, useful, or valuable?

I also want to emphasize three additional points. The first is that to forgive is not to forget. Forgiveness is the gift we give ourselves. It is not dependent on another person doing anything. Second, to forgive is not a signal that we want to try and rebuild trust with that person who betrayed us. That is a different decision. Third, I want to mention that sometimes the person you choose to forgive may no longer be living. That really doesn't matter. The act of forgiveness is important regardless.

I have heard many accounts about how people have gone through the act of forgiveness. Some have an internal conversation and declare their forgiveness. Some say it out loud. Some tell another person. Some write an email or letter (and often then hit "Delete" or tear it up). Some go through some sort of ritual, such as burning their forgiveness letter or casting the torn-up pieces into the wind. You have to determine what is right for you so that you can move to step 7.

- **Step 7 – Let go and move on.** Many people tell me that they have moved on from all kinds of betrayals. I'll then ask the question about their reactions to hearing someone talk about that person; their reaction when they see that person coming toward them in the hallway or in the cafeteria; or their reaction when they see the person's name pop up on their phone. More often than not, I get similar responses: "I avoid them." "I don't answer the phone." "My jaw tightens." If these are your responses, you may not quite have "let go and moved on."

Let's dig a little deeper. If you have a minor, unintentional betrayal, you may not need to work through these seven steps. Or maybe you can work through them quickly, let go, and move on. I strongly recommend that if you have experienced any kind of major betrayal, that you work through the seven steps. By working through each step, your capacity for trusting others is increased. You can become cynical or jaded if you ignore or suppress the betrayals—it's a slippery slope toward trusting no one and, in the most extreme case, paranoia.

Another aspect of the graphic describing the seven steps is that it is a spiral and not a straight line. Depending on the size and complexity of the betrayal, you may think you've completed the first few steps, remember or discover something, and then you have to start again at step 1. Some major betrayals took me years to work through before I could truly move on. The most important thing is to keep working on it. Remember, this is your work to do, and you are the beneficiary of your work.

IF YOU NEED A MIRROR . . .

You may have been reading this chapter with a mindset of how others are not displaying trust behaviors or how others have betrayed you. If that's the case, I encourage you to reread the chapter while also holding up a mirror. Challenge yourself. How are you displaying (or not displaying) behaviors that build strong, trusting relationships? How might you have betrayed someone, intentionally or unintentionally? In the book *The Five Dysfunctions of a Team,* by Patrick Lencioni, trust is the first dysfunction to remedy. If you are working to build a strong relationship and there is little or no trust, it's like building a house on a shaky or unstable foundation. Focus on building a strong, trustworthy mutual relationship first. It will make everything else easier.

One last point. If you visibly begin to change your behavior—even if it is for the better—others' trust of you may initially decline. Remember the *Trust of Character®* behavior "be consistent." If you are changing your behavior, you are no longer consistent and may seem unpredictable. Here is a story from my corporate world days that encompasses both the personal and the professional side of trust behavior.

> *We were having our annual holiday party. I had been leading a transformational executive development program. We had our most senior executives go through the program. One of the executive's wives came up to me and said, "Marsha, I'm mad at you!" I knew this person pretty well and was taken aback by her comment. I asked, "What*

did I do?" She said, "You know that class you're doing that
John is attending? Well, it's causing me some problems."
I asked, "What kind of problems?" She said, "When John
and I argued in the past, I knew how to win. Now I
can't predict what he is going to do or say, so I've lost my
advantage." I laughed and asked her what she thought
I should do. I expected her to tell me to stop teaching the
class. Instead, she suggested that if I was going to teach the
executives new language, skills, and tools, then I should
also teach those same things to the spouses. Believe it or
not, we did some overview sessions with the spouses (with
great success, I might add).

Improving your skills and abilities for building and sustaining trust is not for the faint of heart. You will be required to confront tough thoughts and feelings about people, relationships, and situations. It takes courage, support, and practice. The tools and information in this chapter will help you.

REFLECTION:

What are three things you're going to do differently as a result of what you've learned about trust?

1.

2.

3.

CHAPTER 6

SETTING AND MAINTAINING BOUNDARIES

Givers need to set limits because takers rarely do.

~ Rachel Wolchin

One of the recurring themes I see and hear from women around the world is the challenge of setting and maintaining boundaries. I had to learn this the hard way. I haven't always paid attention to the small signals. Pretty early in my career in my first account executive role, I was responsible for renegotiating a contract for a client we had acquired. It was a $250 million contract, and all eyes seemed to be on me. I was one of few female account executives, and this was our largest client in the financial industry. Bottom line, I averaged about one hundred hours per week for ten months negotiating this contract. Shortly thereafter, I was knocked flat on my back with severe vertigo. I was "down" for seven weeks. I couldn't sit up without falling over, the room was constantly spinning, and I was nauseous most of the time.

As I write this, I am reminded how crazy this time was. "How does this relate to boundaries?" you might ask. I didn't set realistic time frames—what we could and couldn't do in a reasonable period of time. I said "yes" to everything. I didn't delegate. I thought I had to do it all myself. I didn't ask for help. My life was totally out of balance around family, sleep, diet, and exercise. Not only was it hard on me, but I had an amazing team of dedicated people who were right there with me. We laughed at the fact that we knew people's sleeping and snoring patterns, as we slept at our desks on more than one occasion. And, let me be clear, this story has a whole lot more to do with the choices I made than those that were imposed upon me. I had a lot more options on how to manage requests and timelines than I thought I did at that time. Yes, I learned a tremendous amount from the experience, and the relationships formed are still in place today—even with my clients. And, I wouldn't do it that way ever again. In fact, I've never done it that way again. As you read through this chapter, know you have choices, and exercise them effectively, taking YOU into account. I'll give you tangible tools, language, and process steps to help you set and maintain boundaries.

You will recall that "establishing boundaries" is one of the *Trust of Character*® behaviors. When we don't establish boundaries, we betray ourselves; this is also an example of how we give away our power.

MANAGING BOUNDARIES

The conversations I have with women often center around some form of work-life balance. We are juggling so many responsibilities across the spectrums of our lives as wives, mothers, daughters, sisters, friends, employees, bosses, mentors . . . and the list goes on. We must do the hard work to achieve the balance we seek. This brings us back to choices.

As American singer-songwriter, actor, and businesswoman Dolly Parton is fond of saying: "Never get so busy making a living that you forget to make a life."

We have bought into the myth that we women are supposed to do all things for all people and do them really well. And, if we don't, guilt sets in, and we're back to the self-talk of "we're not enough." It happens so frequently that the story grows roots and becomes part of our identity. Busting the myth that we have to do it all in order to be successful is an important lesson to learn no matter our age, generation, or country.

Based on my anecdotal view, with over fifty years of work experience, I find that women are often working on the many, and men are working on the few. Can you relate to that? Do you do all the research and put the "deck" together and the man delivers it and gets a lot of credit? Do you get all the tedious and lengthy to-do list tasks done so someone else can focus on the high-visibility, strategic projects? You'll notice that in the Managing Boundaries framework that Personal Clarity is in the center. Let's start there.

MANAGING PRIORITIES

The following story or fable included in Stephen R. Covey's book *First Things First* has been seen and read by many. I summarize it here to illustrate the importance of prioritizing.

PERSONAL CLARITY: "THE BIG ROCKS OF LIFE" STORY BY DR. STEPHEN R. COVEY

A speaker was presenting to a group of business students. He used an activity to make an important point. He placed a large wide-mouth jar on the table. He then placed fist-sized rocks into the jar until he could no longer fit any more in. He asked the class, "Is the jar full?" It seemed clear that since he could no longer fit any more rocks in that the jar was surely full. Thus a resounding "yes!"

The speaker stated, "Really?" He then proceeded to bring out a pitcher of gravel and poured it into the jar. He asked the students again if the jar was full. The class was a little more cautious, and there was a mix of responses. He then pulled out a pitcher of sand and then water and filled up the jar. The class was now on to him.

He then asked the class what the point of the exercise was. One bright student responded, "The point is that no matter how full your schedule is, if you try really hard you can always fit more things into it."

"No", the speaker replied, "that's not the point. The truth this illustration teaches us is: If you don't put the big rocks in first, you'll never get them in at all."

Leadership Message: "Always put the big rocks in first."

There are so many key messages in this story:

- Can you take your personal and professional objectives and categorize them into Big Rocks, Gravel, Sand, Water?

- Have you stepped back to get clear?

- Have you shared your Big Rocks with the other people in your life?

- Do you allocate your time, energy, and focus on the objectives that really matter to you?

The following activity invites you to look at both Personal and Professional Big Rock priorities. Things to consider as you fill out your list:

- There are seven lines in each column. You don't have to write seven answers in each.

- Generally speaking, think about three to seven important goals you want to ensure you accomplish in the next year.

- Be as precise as you can. For example, don't just write "family" in the "Personal" column; instead, think about what, specifically, you want to accomplish regarding your family.

- Fast-forward to a year from now. You're reflecting on the past year. What will fill your heart with a sense of accomplishment?

IDENTIFYING "BIG ROCKS"

ACTIVITY:

Personal	Professional
1.	1.
2.	2.
3.	3.
4.	4.
5.	5.
6.	6.
7.	7.

Let's do a quick reflection. Was that exercise hard? Easy? Have you ever done anything like this? I try to do this at the beginning of every year. It is yet another tool in my tool kit that guides me in allocating my time and energy. Here is another activity that extends the benefit of the previous exercise.

ACTIVITY:

What criteria did you use to designate your Big Rocks?

If you shared this list with your family or boss, would they agree these were your Big Rocks?

How can you get clarity and alignment with the people in your life around these Big Rocks?

What is the value to you if you allocate your time and energy to these Big Rocks?

continued

What are the next steps you need to take to activate your list, to make it happen?

How will you hold yourself accountable?

How often do you want to review it throughout the next year?
Monthly? Quarterly?

What is the value to your boss, team, and family or loved ones if you allocate your time and energy to these Big Rocks?

Remember, this list is not etched in stone. Even with the best planning efforts, things happen that require you to adjust and shift. Give yourself grace. Don't let the little things distract you. Make sure that any adjustments you make are warranted for significant reasons. Identifying your decision criteria will help you.

MANAGING TIME

How we allocate our time is extremely important. When we start looking at how to better balance our lives, we often think of time management. My hope is that the personal clarity of the activities you just completed will provide a basis for how you allocate your time. You may have heard the expression that states, "If you want to know what people really value, look at their calendar and their checkbook." How an individual spends their time and money tells you a great deal about what is important to them. What would your calendar tell others about what is important to you?

7 PORTS OF LIFE

I have another tool for you to help you more intentionally manage your time. This one is called the "7 Ports of Life" and is included in a group of tools called Model-netics. I learned this tool about forty years ago, and it has been invaluable ever since in a number of ways. The objective of this tool is to examine, in a more detailed way, how we spend our time, with the goal of getting more conscious and intentional about how we allocate it. In addition, and with this consciousness, we can build a target objective on how we want to spend our time in order to live our values and our Big Rock priorities.

Following is a table that reflects the seven ports: Sleep, Work, Family, Social, Spiritual, Community, and Self.

ACTIVITY:

7 Ports of Life	Current Allocation of Time	Desired Allocation of Time	Notes
Sleep			
Work			
Family			
Social			
Spiritual			
Community			
Self			
TOTAL	720 Hours	720 Hours	

Adapted by Marsha Clark & Associates. Source: Model-Netics, Main Event Management.

Look back over the last 30 days and categorize how you spent your time in the Current Allocation of Time column. Hours need to add up to 720 (24 hours/day x 30 days). Here are some explanations on how to think about each category.

Sleep

This is fairly straightforward. How many hours per night do you sleep? I read so many articles, review the research, and hear health and wellness professionals speak on the importance of sleep, because sleep deprivation is a real thing for so many women I know and work with. We're juggling work and home responsibilities. We're trying to get our to-do list completed. We go into power-surge mode and muscle our way through it. What often suffers? Sleep. While each of us may require different amounts of sleep, this chart from the National Sleep Foundation recommends how much sleep we should get based on our age group.

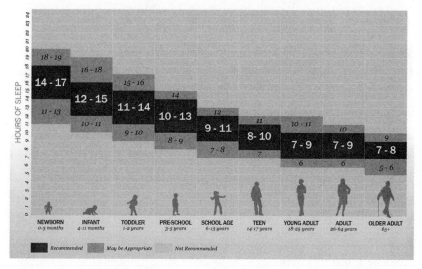

Family

This is a broad category. As you calculate your hours, include grocery shopping, preparing meals, helping with homework, parent-teacher conferences, laundry, housecleaning, clothes shopping for others, family vacations, date night, movie night, and visiting with parents, siblings, and grandparents. Obviously, the time allotted to each may vary month to month. Holiday times, summertime, or school starting can reflect significantly more family needs. Understanding your personal habits or rituals will bring greater consciousness and intentionality in this category.

Work

This category encompasses activities such as getting dressed in the mornings, commuting to and from the office or place of employment, perhaps travel time if your job requires that, and the actual time spent at work. It also includes client dinners, work conferences, networking happy hours, and pulling out the laptop after the kids go to bed. I have used this particular port to dive a little deeper into how I spend my time.

When I started my own business over twenty years ago, I had just left a large Fortune 50 company. You might imagine that there were lots of sophisticated processes and practices to ensure that Fortune 50 company had an efficient, effective, and predictable way of working around the world. My habits were deeply ingrained, and I approached my work by relying on these processes and practices.

I started my business as a solo entrepreneur. One day my husband, after watching me spend hours developing my time-tracking system, asked me why I was spending my time developing all of that, since I was the only employee. When he asked that question, it seemed so clear that there was no need to do all that. So I then broke down the work I needed to do to be a successful businesswoman and entrepreneur, and in my line of work, that was designing, developing, and delivering programs and services. I also had to do marketing and selling, as well as administrative tasks. Spending so much time on non-revenue-producing activities did not bode well for the future sustainability of my business.

How will you categorize your work? You might use your Big Rock priorities. You might also think about it in terms of strategy, operations, client relations, finance, and staff development. The people reading this book will have many different roles. Do what works for you.

Social

It's party time or maybe girlfriend time. Spending time with friends often falls off the calendar when we get so busy. It would be nice to take in a movie, go on a date, join a book club, have lunch with a friend, or maybe host a dinner party. I encourage you to carve out some time to laugh and enjoy time with friends.

Spiritual

This category includes attending church, temple, mosque, or other services. In today's world, this may be done in person or on a virtual platform. If you do volunteer work on behalf of your religion, add that to this category. For others, you may have spiritual practices such as reading materials, prayers, or even journaling.

Community

For most of us this would be some sort of philanthropic activity. Maybe you volunteer at a favorite nonprofit whose mission you support. For others, you may run for a public office in addition to your professional job. If you're a member of your neighborhood's homeowner's association or your Chamber of Commerce, add those hours to this category.

I want to add something that I think is important as you think about your community hours. At different stages of your career, this may not have significant hours allocated to it. Please don't feel guilty about that. When I was traveling almost 100 percent of the time, I didn't have much time to volunteer, no matter how much I might have wanted to do that. Someone from a nonprofit organization told me that there are two ways to contribute—by volunteering our time or writing a check. I was able to write checks and feel better about making a desired contribution. Both are important and appreciated. And to be realistic, there were often times when I could do neither. Maybe it takes every penny to cover the expenses. Or maybe I've had some unexpected expenses. That is absolutely okay. This is a very personal decision. Do what makes sense for you, your time and financial capabilities, and what reinforces your values and priorities.

Self

By talking about self last, I am not suggesting we should be last on our list. I strongly emphasize to women the difference between self and selfish. It is not a selfish act to replenish yourself. Imagine yourself as a vessel. You give and give until you are empty. You are depleted. You have nothing left to give. It is time to refuel in order to have the capacity to continue giving to others. That is not a selfish act. You wouldn't think of driving your car until it ran out of gas. It wouldn't be useful anymore, and neither are you when you are depleted. At that point, we begin to have health issues, relationship issues, or burnout. Please, please, please take care of yourself.

Most women I know enjoy doing for and being with others. If you don't take care of yourself, you will have nothing left to give anyone else. I repeat, it is *not* selfish to take time to replenish. Maybe it's time to read a fun book, do a hobby or craft you enjoy, take a bubble bath, get your nails done, go for a walk or run, work out, or just take a nap. Take care of YOU—make time and keep it!

REFLECTION:

How do you feel about your distribution of hours?

Does your distribution support your value system? Your Big Rock priorities?

Does your distribution reflect a typical thirty-day period or is there something unusual happening (e.g., holidays, summer vacation, year-end close work responsibilities, a big work project, school starting or ending, or a family crisis)? Be as realistic as you can.

What do you think needs to be adjusted? Once you determine those changes, if any, record your "Desired Allocation of Time" in the third column.

In the Notes column, what do you want to capture? The basis of your categorization? Some people use the Notes column to capture reminders or prompts to ensure they are staying true to their Desired Allocation of Time.

Now that you have greater awareness about how you spend your time, shift your thinking to the future. If you are happy with your allocation or categorization, good for you and keep up the great work! If you're not so happy with your allocation, think about what you want it to be for the next 30 days.

Remember, as much as we all wish we could add more hours to the day, we can't. What that means is that if you want more hours in one category, you must reduce the number of hours in another category. All the hours still need to add up to 720.

THOUGHTS TO CONSIDER

Even though you can't add hours to a day, you can leverage or optimize the hours spent, basically getting "credit" in several ports or categories. For example, you can do social activities or community activities with other family members or friends. When my son was young, our family supported the nonprofit Special Olympics. My husband would referee at a weekend basketball tournament. My son was water boy for both teams, and I would register teams and help people get to the right gym. We were filling several ports. We did this as a family supporting our community, and each of us felt good about our individual roles. It supported our values, and my son and his wife are now teaching their children in similar ways.

You must be deliberate and diligent about honoring your Desired Allocation of Time. I encourage you to review the actual allocation of your hours on a Friday afternoon for the preceding week. How close were you? If not close, what caused the variance? Remember, give yourself grace. Building new habits and creating this kind of discipline is hard and takes time. On that same Friday afternoon, take a look at the upcoming week. Does your schedule support your Desired Allocation of Time? Do you need to make adjustments?

Don't be afraid to ask for help or put prompts in place to help you carry out your plan. Review your actual and desired hours along with your needed adjustments with your family, loved ones, and colleagues, and ask for their help in making it happen. An added benefit is that you're giving them permission to do the same. Maybe you can set an alarm for when it's time to leave the office or as a cue for when to put away the work and go to sleep. And if you need to "just finish this one thing" when the alarm goes off, hit "snooze" rather than "stop" so you'll get another alarm reminder.

You can do this. Work to make a few small adjustments rather than trying to overhaul your entire life. If you want to get more sleep, try going to bed fifteen minutes earlier for a month. If you hold true to it, you'll get 7.5 more hours of sleep in a month. And that's like an extra night's sleep—woohoo! I bet you'll feel better. After you've developed a few new habits or practices, add a few more.

MANAGING WORK

Another big challenge I hear from my clients is about how hard it is to truly delegate. "It's easier to do it myself." "It takes less time for me to do it myself than the time required to teach them to do it." "They don't do it the way I like to do it." Sound familiar? You will reach a point when you just can't get it all done. There aren't enough hours in a day.

As you move through your career, you may shift from being *solely* responsible for getting the task or project done to *ensuring* that the task or project gets done. Read that sentence again. As a leader, it is your responsibility to *ensure* that the task or project gets done. In other words, you don't have to do it yourself. To delegate is to commit or entrust to another. Delegation is a tool for developing others, giving them an opportunity to gain knowledge and perspective, planning and follow-through skills, and the importance of communication and accountability. Those are important things for each of us to learn. You don't want to deprive others of such learning and development.

Here is a tool or framework that will help you know when to delegate and how to ensure the task or project will be completed successfully. This is another tool from Model-netics that I've been using for about forty years.

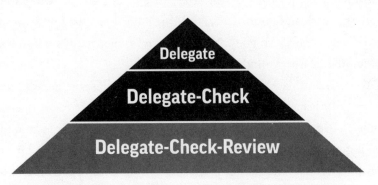

Source: Model-Netics, Main Event Management. Adapted by Marsha Clark & Associates.

DELEGATE-CHECK-REVIEW

It is a pretty straightforward approach. You **delegate** the task and provide the requirements and expectations. You set up a cadence of periodic meetings to **check** on progress and adherence to the requirements and expectations. Last, you **review** the output or results before sending it to the client, boss, colleague, or whoever requested the task or project.

The variables for you to consider when selecting this approach are:

- **It's a long-term project.** This kind of project requires more research, activities, meetings, departments, and people. By setting up a cadence of periodic meetings and checks, you ensure that the project stays on course relative to time and delivery. If it does get off-course, more frequent checks can bring it back in line with less rework.

- **It's a high-visibility project.** If you will have a lot of senior-level people, clients, community, or marketplace people interested in and tracking the progress or status of the project, you want to ensure a frequent and thorough check-and-review process.

- **It's a high-risk project.** A project can be high risk if it is complex; you have never done anything like it before; you have fewer experienced people involved; several groups, clients, or teams are involved; or if it is costly. Expenses can include capital spending, large staff expenditures, or global implementation. The amount of risk is relative to the organization's revenue or size. What's high risk to one organization may be low risk to another. Once again, the answer is, "It depends." You will have to determine whether your project is a high-risk one or not.

- **Working with new people.** There are two kinds of "new people." The first kind includes those you have worked with but who are new to this kind of work. They may have related experience or maybe they have done similar projects that were smaller in scope. You may have several on the staff who have less experience working on your project, or none at all. The second kind is someone who is new to you. Perhaps they have done similar work in another part of your organization or even in a different organization. You have never worked with them directly and are doing so for the first time. Whichever of these two kinds of employees reflects your situation, you need to set up an appropriate check-and-review process.

And this leads us to another tool for our tool kit—the **Checks & Balances Tool**.

This is a tool I have used for many years. It allows you to share with your boss, client, or stakeholder the status of the project at an executive-level view, as well as allowing you to review with your assigned project leader so you have adequate and timely information to ensure effective project tracking. This tool will help you delegate with greater confidence, assuming you employ it in a weekly review process or cadence.

Some things to note as you begin to use this tool. It is intended to be a one-page check-and-review document. By following this guideline, you better ensure that you are not micromanaging the project or getting "too much into the weeds." By using this consistent format, review meetings are typically more efficient and effective. You get the critical information you need and are less likely to get distracted by extraneous information.

CHECKS AND BALANCES TOOL:

What did I accomplish in this period?	What are my objectives for the next period?
What are my challenges/issues/obstacles?	What are key metrics? Progress, to date?

A more detailed explanation of what to include in each quadrant is as follows:

Quadrant 1: What did I accomplish this period? – This quadrant reflects all that has been accomplished in the last week. Accomplishments might include research completed, processes documented, key meetings, milestone deliverables, and any critical path items (things that must be complete before the next task can be completed).

Quadrant 2: What are my objectives for the next period? – This quadrant reflects the objectives or tasks for the coming week; the things that will need to be accomplished to keep the project on schedule. Ideally, this Quadrant 2 will be transferred to Quadrant 1 when moving from week to week. If, for some reason, a task is not completed, move it to Quadrant 1 and note as much. Highlighting or placing an asterisk behind it allows it to be tracked more closely. It also helps from a Quadrant 3 perspective.

Quadrant 3: What are my challenges/issues/obstacles? – This quadrant identifies anything that prevents objectives from being achieved for the previous review period or the upcoming one. When the project leader reviews this update with the client/boss/stakeholder, they will first share what they have done to address the challenge. The project leader needs to make sure they are not waiting for others to solve their problems for them. If you are the boss/client/stakeholder, this is where you want to maintain boundaries and hold your project leader accountable and further develop their critical thinking and problem-solving skills. Coach them on next steps and encourage them to take ownership. Ask them what they need from you to address the challenge or issue. Work hard to teach them how to remove obstacles before bringing them to you.

Quadrant 4: What are key metrics? Progress, to date? – This quadrant identifies key measures for progress or success in project completions. It may reflect percentages, budget dollars, time, deadlines met, or key deliverables based on agreed-upon success factors. Ideally, these would be agreed upon when the delegated task or project is initiated. Adjustments may need to be made as the project evolves. Make sure delegated tasks are aligned and everyone is clear on success factors.

Let me wrap up describing this tool with a few more thoughts.

- This consistent, structured tool enables a leader to review, align, and assess appropriate performance against an employee's goals, objectives, projects, and day-to-day responsibilities.

- This tool assists in holding employees accountable based on a consistent pattern of documented performance.

- This tool is reviewed during one-on-one meetings that are typically held weekly or biweekly.

- This tool is critical in maintaining alignment regarding project deliverables and measures for success. When used consistently, it can prevent projects (and employees) from getting too far "off course" so that adjustments can be made to get things back on track.

- It is a great tool for building trust in terms of managing expectations and following through on commitments, as well as accountability regarding an employee's performance.

- Maintaining these reports over a given performance period (quarterly, semiannually, annually) allows the leader to provide timely feedback and documentation.

- This tool is very useful when preparing for an employee's midyear and annual performance review.

Now let's move to the Delegate-Check portion of the triangle.

Adapted by Marsha Clark & Associates. Source: Model-Netics, Main Event Management.

DELEGATE-CHECK

You **delegate** the task or project and provide the requirements and expectations. You set up your cadence of periodic meetings to **check** on progress and adherence to the requirements and expectations. You are comfortable enough with the person to whom you have delegated as well as with your periodic checkpoints that you don't have to review every output before it is shared with stakeholders.

The key variables to consider are:

- **Is it a midterm project** (more than a month but less than three months)?

- **Is it a medium or average visibility project** (one or two stakeholder groups involved in oversight or receiving the output)?

- **Are you working with familiar people** (people with whom you've worked before and whose expertise you trust on this particular type of project)?

And finally, let's review the top of the triangle.

Adapted by Marsha Clark & Associates. Source: Model-Netics, Main Event Management.

DELEGATE

These are tasks or projects where you **delegate** them and then practically forget about them. Admittedly, these examples include delegating to people you *know*, *love*, and *trust*.

Variables to consider are:

- **Is it an immediate task or project** with a short turnaround time?

- Is it **a low-visibility task or project** (one person needs the information or deliverable)?

- **Is it a low-risk task or project** (it's familiar, routine, or readily available information or deliverable)?

- **Are you delegating the task or project to someone you trust** (you have a positive track record with this person following through with quality work or results, or the person has considerable experience doing the delegate task or project)?

Now you are ready to delegate. As leadership training coach Craig Groeschel sagely states, "If you delegate tasks, you create followers; if you delegate authority, you create leaders."

REFLECTION

What are three things you are currently doing that you can delegate to some-one else?

1.

2.

3.

THOUGHTS TO CONSIDER

- If you and one of your direct reports are both attending the same meeting, delegate attending the meeting to your direct report. Communicate this decision to the meeting organizer and share your reasoning. Ensure that your direct report shares a summary of the meeting with you. For example, key messages, decisions made, any commitments impacting you or your team, key deadlines and deliverables, and applicable next steps. This review should take no more than fifteen minutes. If the delegated meeting is a one-hour weekly meeting, you just reclaimed three hours per month. I strongly encourage you to be intentional about what you do with this time. Do you want to spend it doing more strategic thinking or planning? More time working on Big Rock priorities? More time coaching and developing your team? More time with your family or loved ones? Don't let it get lost on trivial tasks.

- Are there periodic reports that someone on your team could complete? Coach them on how to do it. Give them access to the information as applicable. Notify anyone involved who is used to dealing with you. Check the report the first few times to ensure accuracy. Again, be intentional with how you choose to use the newfound time.

- When you delegate to one of your team members, consider how the task or project will benefit them. Does it teach them new skills? Do they get to showcase their talents? Does it broaden their network and visibility or contribute to their career goals? Developmental assignments are one of the best learning experiences. Make the connection for people that you are delegating a task or project for developmental purposes (and make sure you really and truly are!), and identify how it will be developmental.

- Consider what you might want to delegate in your personal life. For example, are your children old enough to pack their own lunches or do their own laundry? And remember to use any newfound time intentionally. I strongly recommend you consider some self-care or replenishment time. Maybe go for a walk, work out, read, or call a friend. You're not being selfish. You are refueling.

MANAGING THE PROCESS

The framework in this Managing the Process section is based on the work of Mark Sachs, organization consultant, executive coach, and my Master's program practicum advisor.

Setting boundaries means we are *taking responsibility for ourselves* and *promoting mutuality and respect in our relationships*. It also means we're setting limits—what we can or will do, as well as what we can't or won't do. Respecting yourself and your time creates an opportunity for you to hold on to your power. And when and where you set boundaries is different depending on the situation. You want to be sure that you honor the commitments you've already made before taking on more commitments, particularly if they require you to sleep less or spend less time with loved ones. (Remember your 7 Ports of Life and your Desired Allocation of Time!)

What is the language of setting boundaries? Here are some examples:

- "This is what I need from you and by this date."
- "No." (I'll come back to this one.)
- "This is what I am willing to do."
- "This is how I want this done."

These are just a few of many. Let's dig a little deeper to understand more.

POSSIBLE SIGNS OF DIFFICULTY WITH SETTING BOUNDARIES

The following information is designed to provide a few cues or warning signals that you may have violated or compromised your boundaries. The first step in ensuring that you maintain healthy boundaries is to create awareness about your weaknesses in this area.

Doing Things You Don't Want to Do for Others

Have you ever found yourself walking away from a conversation or hanging up the phone and thinking, "Why did I just agree to take that on?" Maybe the task or "favor" you have agreed to is not a part of your job responsibilities. Maybe it's work that a more junior person is better suited to do. Maybe it requires extra hours you don't have.

REFLECTION:

Think of a recent example when you may have accepted a task or duty you didn't want to take on.

Discuss what factors made you take it on anyway, and how you felt after agreeing to the work.

If you could go back and say no to the task or duty, what would you say? What can you do to ensure you do not take on assignments you don't have room for?

Avoiding Others

Most of us have one or more people in our lives who are frequently asking us to do something. If you see that person walking down the hall or across the cafeteria, or if you see their name come up on your phone, you may want to escape to the ladies' room, avert eye contact, or let the call go to voice mail.

REFLECTION:

Think of a time when you avoided someone.

Were there "side effects" to your avoidance? Did it end up raising stress levels for you, or increasing tension in the space you share with the individual you avoided?

Feeling Helpless or Powerless

We live in a pressure cooker of "yes" culture. Anything less than a "can-do!" is unacceptable . . . or so we have come to believe. You may find yourself feeling that you have no choice but to say yes. Believing you have no choice is one of the ways you give your power away. Remember, we always have a choice. Sometimes we just have to muster the courage to say no or offer an alternative. You'll be surprised how agreeable the other person is. All those stories you're telling yourself don't come to fruition. Try it. The more experience you have in setting boundaries, the easier it will be.

REFLECTION:

Think of an example when you recently believed you had no choice but to say yes.

In the spirit of "What else could be true?" can you think of other choices you might have had?

Feeling Resentful after We Have Said "Yes"

You say yes and smile at the person who has just made what you consider a somewhat unreasonable request. Or maybe it was reasonable, but you have so much on your plate already. You walk away and grimace at what just happened. You feel increasingly angry with the other person for having the nerve to ask you to do something for them. Don't they realize how busy you are? Then, you get mad at yourself because, once again, you didn't set a boundary and said yes when you wanted to say no.

I don't know about you, but I had to search within and recognize I was contributing to this situation. As long as I kept saying yes, they would keep asking. Only I can change the situation.

REFLECTION:

Think of a time when feeling resentful because of your own inability to say no has impacted work relationships.

How can you manage this differently going forward?

Procrastinating

If you find yourself waiting until the last minute, it may be a sign of difficulty setting boundaries. Ask yourself if you're putting off the task because you didn't want to do it in the first place. Is the job better suited for someone else based on their skills and experience? Do you find yourself resenting the project or the person who asked you to do it? Does the story in your head then shift to how others don't appreciate you or understand how overworked you are? If you find yourself procrastinating on a task, ask yourself if it is connected to you not setting or maintaining a boundary in the first place.

REFLECTION:

Can you think of a recent task you procrastinated on?

How did your procrastination relate to boundary setting?

WHY IT MIGHT BE DIFFICULT FOR YOU TO SET BOUNDARIES

You need to understand what is driving you to not set or maintain boundaries. Then you'll want to challenge your own thinking about it.

Avoiding Conflict

Why can't we all just get along? It's easier for me to say yes to a request than it is to argue or fuss about it. We dread those conversations. But try to imagine the reality—the requester saying "okay" to your "no." They might ask someone else to do it or agree to an alternative timeline for delivery, in most cases without getting their feathers ruffled. Yes, sometimes you will make someone unhappy, and that's okay.

Each of us has our own views about conflict. For some, a harsh tone is difficult for us. Some of us read between the lines and bristle at what we think may be passive-aggressive resentment. Examine your own thoughts about conflict. Recognize that you're assuming a conflict, and that is only one possibility. Say no and see what happens. Notice what you are thinking and how you're feeling. What happened? How will that inform your decisions in future situations?

Fear of Being Perceived as Incompetent or a Poor Team Player

If you say no or provide an alternative, will the requester think you don't have the skills or experience to do the task? Or might they think you're not being a good team player? The real answer is, "It depends." Do you say no every time you're asked? Is there, in fact, a more qualified person who could fulfill the request more efficiently and effectively? Later in this chapter, I'll discuss how you can respond to a request and minimize a reaction that assumes incompetence or that you're being a poor team player.

Disapproval

Maybe you fear that people won't like you or you will damage a relationship. I daresay that it is not a very solid relationship if it is primarily based on you saying yes to everything that is asked of you. It is certainly not a mutually respectful relationship.

Not Wanting to Inconvenience Others

I cringe as I think of this situation. So, it's okay to inconvenience you but not okay for anyone or everyone else to be inconvenienced? Are you sure? I have seen scenarios where people are treated as doormats—walked over, trampled again and again. Then the requester declares the person lacks self-esteem, self-confidence, or self-worth. Whoa, wait a minute! I'm pretty sure that is not your problem or your intent.

These requests or your responses are not always happening at a conscious level. I encourage you to get clear about how you want to show up. You don't have to declare that your time is important, too. For many, that will be received as harsh or even combative. Declaring that you already have commitments and deadlines to meet is a way of communicating both your sense of responsibility and follow-through, as well as your ability to manage your workload, ensuring you have the balance you need and desire. It's okay to take yourself into account as you choose your response.

Career Repercussions

If you say no, will it have a negative impact on your career opportunities? Once again, it depends. Are they asking you to work this weekend or asking you to take a role and relocate your family to another country? Consider the pattern of your responses. Are you clear about your desired career direction? Is the ask one that could advance your career? Is it a good or bad time to make a move with your family? If you say "no" every time, they likely will stop asking after a while.

I have coached people—both men and women—on this. I advise them to tell their superiors that they are declining the opportunity at this time, for these reasons, and then to say, "Please ask me again should another opportunity arise." That being said, regardless of the impact you saying "no" may have, sometimes you will have to prioritize. Maybe you want to allow your children to finish high school at their current school. Maybe your parents are aging and you want to be close by to look in on them and spend quality time with them. Maybe your spouse or partner can't relocate given their career aspirations or based on current responsibilities.

Just make sure you honor both your personal and professional values and Big Rock priorities. Let the appropriate people know. It is rare that there is only one opportunity. Another will likely come along at the right time for you to say yes.

SETTING BOUNDARIES

- **Step 1** – You must first get clear about what your boundaries are. We often discover our boundaries *after* someone has crossed them. In the previous section, you identified patterns of difficulty setting and maintaining boundaries. From that list, can you begin to develop your set of boundaries?

  There may be some boundaries you will never compromise. For example, don't ask me to violate my values—misrepresenting information to a client to cover up our own mistake. Others are situational boundaries based upon your current workload and commitments, ensuring you have your desired work-life balance, your health, or your personal situation. Be prepared to say what you will or won't do or what you can or can't do. It is better if you say this earlier rather than later in the process of requesting and getting it done. Don't miss a deadline or fall short on a commitment because you took on more than you could handle. I encourage you to be as direct as possible in your response. You don't have to make excuses, go on and on, or feel guilty about setting and maintaining a boundary.

- **Step 2** – It's important to be consistent. Once you've set a boundary, be sure you follow through and maintain the commitment. There are people in our lives both personally and professionally who will try to wear us down. They will keep asking us again and again. Maybe they give you that look or use that tone. They may attempt to heap guilt on you. Stay strong. The goal is a mutually respectful relationship. Chilling looks, harsh tones, or guilting language does not reflect a mutually respectful relationship.

- **Step 3** – Just as you want to hold yourself accountable for maintaining your boundaries, you want to hold others accountable as well. Be clear when communicating your boundary as well as any consequences of honoring or not honoring your boundary. For example, you might set a curfew for a child to be home. What are the consequences if they consistently meet or don't meet the curfew? The same can be applied to employees or team members who do or do not meet clear deadlines.

- **Step 4** – Look for patterns in your own or others' lives. Remember, a dot is a dot, two dots a line, three dots a trend. Identifying patterns helps you better manage your response and your actions. You can anticipate a request coming. For example, let's say it's time to develop the annual budget or operating plan, and you know you'll be asked to do all the research and your boss will present it. Is it time to give someone else this developmental opportunity? Or it's the holiday season and you are being asked to host the extended family for a big dinner. Do you love doing it, or does all the preparation, work, and cleanup fall on you? Will you set some boundaries around what you will and won't do? Maybe you ask others to bring favorite foods and you assign a cleanup crew that doesn't include you. This will give you an opportunity to enjoy the time to visit with family members, too.

- **Step 5** – And last but certainly not least, thank the other person for honoring your boundary or honoring their commitment. Your acknowledgment reinforces the boundary and lets them know you are serious. We generally like being thanked or acknowledged, and it encourages us to repeat the behavior.

Remember

We've covered a lot of material so far, and we're not quite done. This is a far-reaching topic that requires depth and breadth. I want to share some concepts to remember and practice.

- I will say it again, **"We teach people how to treat us."** If they ask and you keep saying yes, they will keep asking you. Count on it.

- **"No" is a complete sentence.** Your need to explain, defend, rationalize, or apologize is not always needed or necessary. Women have told me this is the hardest thing for them to do. Then they try it and tell me it felt really good. All the negative stories they had told themselves did not play out. They discovered a "What else could be true?" moment in real time.

- **Separate the recognition from the request.** My favorite example of this principle sounds like this:

    > *Jennifer, I want to thank you for leading our local dona-*
    > *tion project!*
    >
    > *Our organization raised more money this year than*
    > *ever before. Your creativity and planning as the leader*
    > *of the initiative made all the difference. I was so proud*
    > *walking on to the stage to accept the recognition for our*
    > *organization's contributions. So many in our community*
    > *will be helped by the donations you helped us to collect. I*
    > *know you have even more great ideas about how to do*
    > *even better next year. I can count on you to lead the initia-*
    > *tive next year, right?*

    I typically walk up to a woman in class and go through this dialogue. In almost every situation the woman says "yes." She is often blushing and is almost embarrassed with all of the praise

I'm heaping on her. How could she not say "yes"? And this leads to my next point.

- **You don't always have to give an immediate response.** This is a great place to slow down and get clear before responding. Give yourself the time to be intentional in your response. Here is my recommendation for your in-the-moment response (and my wish for you is that it becomes your new default response):

    I am proud of the leadership I provided on this great initiative, and I had a great team to work with (Remember: "I + we"). As I'm sure you know, this takes a lot of extra hours to make it happen and achieve the kind of results we enjoyed. I will need to take a look at my current projects, timelines, and commitments before I respond. Let me get back to you in a few days.

- This leads to the next potential response. **Consider a "soft no" and offer another option or alternative.** Following on the previous interaction, you have now reviewed your commitments and have made the decision not to take on the initiative for a second year.

    I have had an opportunity to look at my current workload and commitments and have decided not to take on this philanthropic initiative. I have a recommendation for someone that I think can offer great leadership to this initiative and for whom it would be a great developmental assignment. Whoever you might select, I am also happy to turn over my notes and share my thoughts with them. I'll also be available for thirty days to answer any questions the initiative leader might have.

I want to highlight some key points on this example. You are clear that you take your commitments seriously. You offer an alternative to be helpful. You stress that it is a developmental opportunity. And you set another boundary by being available for thirty days. This last point is really important. I have experienced personally and heard as a coach that you say no, and then you end up doing the role anyway, and you get no credit or recognition for doing so. That is a lose-lose for you. This is a great example of *maintaining* the boundary. In this scenario, turn over your notes. Remind the new initiative leader when the thirty days is up. If that person continues coming back to you, let them know it is their call to make or that they can find that information in the notes you passed along. If you keep giving them the answers, they'll keep coming to you with questions. This is tough *and* you can do it. At the end of the initiative, congratulate them on their good work.

- The next point was given to me by my good friend, Dottie Gandy. **It is easier to say no when there is a bigger yes burning inside.** What is your bigger yes? Think about your values, your Big Rocks, your health, and your time with family and loved ones. Consider your bigger yes before you respond and remember your new default language, "Let me take a look at my current commitments and I'll get back to you," before responding. Slow down, be clear, and be intentional.

- I learned this next point from a quality workshop that I attended many years ago. It didn't make sense to me when I first heard it, and I have since seen it play out many times in the way they taught us. The point is: **"There is freedom through boundaries."** My first reaction when I heard it was "no way." Boundaries are limits, so how can there be freedom in limits? Then they shared this study that was done.

There are two identical schoolhouses. Each one has the same playground behind the school with an open field beyond the playground. The only difference is that one playground has a fence around it (a boundary) and the other doesn't. The bell rings and the children come out to the playground for recess.

I have shared this example in my programs. I will ask the class if they think there are any differences in how the children play in the playground area based on fence or no fence.

The responses reflect that the majority of participants believe there is more freedom to be found in the unfenced playground. A few, however, assert that there is more freedom to be found in the fenced-in playground. It comes as no surprise that the latter response comes from the teachers and principals that have likely had firsthand experience in observing this.

Bottom line, the study showed that with no fence, the children hovered closer to the school building. In contrast, the children played freely throughout the entire area in the fenced-in playground. They felt freer knowing that this is the area where they could safely play. It isn't too big a leap to see how this is analogous to our adult work world. When you set boundaries, our teams can "play" freely within those boundaries. Examples are setting clear expectations as well as communicating and aligning on those expectations. "Here is what is expected or acceptable. Here is what is not expected or acceptable."

- Rounding out these key points to consider is a question that one of my program participants gave me many years ago. **"Can I continue to do this with love in my heart?"** Isn't that a great question? No resentment. No guilt. No blame or judgment. I have love in my heart as I complete the task or activities you've requested. Maybe you love hosting that holiday dinner at your house. If you can do that year after year with love in your heart, then by all means, go for it.

• And last, I would like to offer a few key items to remember. First, the definition of insanity is doing the same thing you've always done over and over again and somehow expecting a different result. In other words, you can't keep saying "yes" and taking on unwanted work, yet expect or hope that others will miraculously stop asking. And second, the more often you are successful at setting and maintaining boundaries, the easier it will get!

SUMMARY

We have covered a great deal of material in this chapter. You have gained clarity regarding your Big Rocks or priorities both personally and professionally. You have identified how you want to allocate your precious time. You have identified some tasks, meetings, or projects that you will delegate with confidence, as you now have a framework and the corresponding and appropriate checks and balances. You have some guidance on the process and language of setting and maintaining boundaries. Let's bring it all together.

REFLECTION:

What have you learned about yourself and your default patterns when it comes to setting and maintaining boundaries?

What are some new behaviors or language you're going to use going forward?

Who do you need to have a conversation with to establish new boundaries?

Who is going to hold you accountable for setting and maintaining boundaries (other than yourself)?

What are some upcoming opportunities that would give you a chance to put what you've learned into practice—setting boundaries to ensure a more mutually respectful relationship?

Look at the next ninety days as you consider these opportunities.

Make a note on your calendar every quarter to review and celebrate your progress. Then, set new quarterly goals. Give yourself grace. Old habits and defaults are hard to break. Let people know your goals. Ask for help. Consider an accountability partner who can support you with love and encouragement.

When you are doubting yourself or need to change your self-talk, come back to this page and say aloud these affirmations of your basic rights. You might even want to read them every morning to start your day strong.

AFFIRMATIONS OF BASIC RIGHTS

- I always have the right to be who I am and to stand up for myself.

- I deserve to be treated with dignity and respect.

- I have the right to express what I feel and think, so long as I don't try to tell others what is right for them.

- I accept my right to be imperfect and to do so without feeling guilty.

- No one has the authority to tell me what to feel, what to think, or what to do.

- If I stand up for myself, I will have more courage, and I will be happier. The future will be brighter and better for me in the long run.

CHAPTER 7

TRUSTING YOUR INTUITION

The best leaders are readers of people. They have the
intuitive ability to understand others by discerning
how they feel and recognizing what they sense.

~ John C. Maxwell

The information in this chapter is based on LaRue Eppler's work in intuition. LaRue is an intuition coach, speaker, and author who has been helping clients around the world for over thirty years. She is the creator of The Evo-K Method and Evo-K Coach Certification Program, a revolutionary technology for personal growth and inner transformation. In 2008, LaRue co-authored *Your Essential Whisper*, a book on intuition with in-depth guidance on how to recognize, trust, and follow inner guidance with absolute certainty.

Trusting my intuition may have saved my life. As a bit of context, I have been blessed with very good health as well as a high tolerance for pain. One day, I began itching over almost all of my body. I figured that I had come in contact with something that was causing my body to react. I went to the drugstore and talked to the pharmacist—I didn't have a primary care physician because I was so healthy. The pharmacist gave me some topical cream and told me if the itching didn't subside in a few days, I should go see a doctor. It didn't go away and I made an appointment at one of the neighborhood clinics. They speculated that I had a gallstone that was causing the bile from my body to back up into my bloodstream, which was what was causing the itching. They scheduled me for a sonogram the next day. The sonogram was my first and lasted about an hour. I understand now that an hour was a pretty lengthy sonogram.

The next day, the clinic physician called and asked me to come back in to hear about the results of my sonogram. Parallel to all this happening, I was scheduled for a business trip to Singapore. I was eager to take care of whatever was wrong and be on my way. I was impatient to say the least. Regardless of this, when the physician insisted I come in, my intuition was screaming at me to listen and heed his instructions—even though it was typical for me to just "grin and bear it" and "deal with it later."

Here is the bottom line: I had a cancerous tumor at the base of my pancreas, and it was causing a blockage in both my ampullary duct as well as my bile duct. I learned that from the clinic physician and was immediately referred to a specialist who almost immediately scheduled me for surgery. Little did I know that there is a 6 percent survival rate from pancreatic cancer. The survival rate is so low because pancreatic cancer is typically asymptomatic. People often don't know they have it until they are Stage 4 and treatment is not effective. I listened to my intuition by going to the pharmacist, then the neighborhood clinic and the specialist, and ultimately to the operating room for a thirteen-hour surgery called the Whipple procedure. I'm happy to say I am now ten years cancer-free and very glad that I listened to and respected my intuition.

Trust your gut. We hear this often, but how do you come to trust something you can't see or have no evidence for?

WHAT IS INTUITION?

Intuition is a natural ability we use every day without realizing it. It goes by many names and is defined by experts in various ways. Some scholars say intuition is digested knowledge that springs to mind when needed.

I'm going to share with you what I refer to as *True Intuition*. True Intuition is knowing something without having any prior experience, knowledge, or understanding about a subject or situation. I'm excited to share Six Distinct Ways intuition communicates with you using your past as a petri dish for exploration. Give yourself permission to explore and practice.

Did you know your heart has beat over 97,000 times in the last twenty-four hours? It beat over four thousand times in the last sixty minutes alone. You certainly don't have to "tell" it what to do. I propose that this higher intelligence is the source of True Intuition. If it knows how to create and suspend planets in space for billions of years, it knows how to help you achieve your goals, protect you from harm, and it even knows why you're here on earth and how to help you achieve your purpose.

True Intuition is simply a "knowing without knowing how you know." Would you like to learn how to partner with it? Keep reading!

THE INTUITIVE LEADER

Being an ardent student of intuition, my ears stand to attention anytime I hear billionaires like media mogul Oprah Winfrey and Starbucks Founder Howard Schultz credit intuition as their guiding light for success and leadership. In 2008, Starbucks' sales were sliding downward at an alarming rate. With the stock price rapidly declining and the company's very survival at risk, Mr. Schultz stepped back in as CEO to save his sinking ship. He detailed the harrowing experience in his book *Onward: How Starbucks Fought for Its Life without Losing Its Soul*, making nineteen direct references to intuition and how he used it to save the company, despite what the experts were advising him to do.

What intrigued me the most was his leadership style. He always maintained a sixth sense about those who would be a good character fit for his company. His optimism about Starbucks had always come from an inner knowing that when they relegated responsibility to leaders, and provided them with the right tools and resources, those leaders would exceed expectations.

Take the story of Mayumi Kitamura, a Starbucks manager in Tokyo, whose store started hosting coffee-tasting parties for customers who are visually impaired. Mayumi and colleagues came up with the idea after a blind customer told them he only ordered drip coffee because that was all he knew to order. After that, they made a Braille menu and kept it right next to the register. Mayumi and her team certainly exceeded expectations.

Intuitive leaders are powerfully aware that they are a small part of a greater whole. Because they can sense and feel deeply, they have the ability to support, inspire, and encourage team members by creating trust and connection between them. They know how to generate an environment of safety that spurs creativity, bringing out their inventive best.

BRIDGING LOGIC AND INTUITION

Forbes magazine once published an article about a Japanese billionaire's approach to making important decisions. He told them *he ate his decisions*, explaining that after the research is finalized and it's time to decide, he eats dinner. If the food digests well and he feels good the next morning, it's a good choice, but if it didn't, it's the wrong choice. Talk about trusting your gut!

We may have all the right data and input, but without tuning in to your intuition, you won't have a gut sense of whether something is *right* or not. The rational mind isn't always the best source of information, because the ego takes control with its overanalyzing, resisting, protecting, and second-guessing. Albert Einstein is quoted as saying, "The intuitive mind is a sacred gift and the rational mind is a faithful servant. We have created a society that honors the servant and has forgotten the gift."

Each person is born with an innate guidance system to help them fulfill their purpose. But, sadly, modern society has put the cart before the horse. They put the rational mind in charge instead of their intuitive guidance system. Why is this so? Academic intelligence has taken top honors, with intuition relegated to the back of the bus.

But this is backward. The rational mind is to be the servant of the soul, letting the soul (intuition) tell the rational mind what to do. Having said that, I believe we need to use both the rational and intuitive mind together in partnership. The rational mind gathers facts while the intuitive mind leads the way. It's the part of you that knows what you know without knowing how you know it. It knows if you're on the right track or not, and what decisions are best for you. The story about the Japanese businessman relying on his digestion is an excellent example of how we can use both the rational and intuitive mind together when making decisions. The hurdles to accessing intuition are often our incessant need for speed—we simply have too many deadlines to slow down and become mindful.

Mindfulness is when you're aware of what you're sensing and feeling in the moment, without interpretation of judgment. It helps you not only recognize your intuition, but also discern it from normal mental chatter. To help slow down the busy mind, use this simple mindfulness technique of taking four to five slow breaths in and out, followed by noticing what you're feeling or sensing. This easy breathing technique is like an inner massage bringing a sense of calm and softer mental chatter, enabling you to tune in to the subtle sensations or feelings you may otherwise be unaware of.

MALE AND FEMALE BRAINS—ARE THEY DIFFERENT?

Many like to say women have superior intuition compared to men, and of course that point is arguable. The expression "women's intuition" is applied by men and women alike. However, there is much debate in the scientific community over whether male and female brains are biologically different or not. Neuroscientist Lise Eliot, a professor of neuroscience at the Chicago Medical School and the author of *Pink Brain, Blue Brain*, says they're more alike than we think.

Dr. Rob Pascale and Dr. Louis Primavera (authors of *Making Marriage Work*) discuss this in their blog, So Happy Together. Researchers propose that wiring differences result in different strengths. Here is a summary of research findings compiled by Dr. Rob Pascale and Dr. Lou Primavera in their article published in *Psychology Today*.

- Men are better at performing single tasks; women are better at multitasking.

- Women are better at attention, word memory and social cognition, and verbal abilities.

- Men are better at spatial processing and sensorimotor speed.[*]

- Women are better at fine-motor coordination and retrieving information from long-term memory.

- Women are more oriented toward and have better memories of faces, and men have better memories of things.

- Men are better at visualizing a two- or three-dimensional shape rotated in space, at correctly determining angles from the horizontal, at tracking moving objects, and at aiming projectiles.

- In finding their way, men rely more on dead reckoning. That is, they determine their position from the direction and distance traveled. Women tend to rely more on landmarks.

If women have more neural connections between their right and left brain, are women more intuitive? The scientific jury is still undecided, but I

---

[*]   Spatial processing, a cognitive process, enables a person to remember different locations as well as spatial relations between objects. Sensorimotor speed is the rate of speed in which the senses detect objects and respond.

can't help but wonder if having more connections between the two hemi-spheres is why women often experience what is called women's intuition.

Regardless of the differences in male and female brains, what I know is that everyone has intuition. With practice, they can maximize their life and profession by utilizing it, so let's dive in to the Six Distinct Ways intuition communicates with you now.

SIX DISTINCT WAYS INTUITION COMMUNICATES

Intuition is with you all the time. It's been with you from the day you were born. Life experiences, however, may have made it hard to rec-ognize and especially challenging to trust. Developing a successful relationship with intuition is like any other relationship you care about. It takes commitment and attention. Intuition wants to partner with you and quickly responds to your commitment to listening to it.

There are six distinct experiences of intuition. With practice, you'll come to discern the subtle nuances of intuition and gain confidence in your ability to recognize, trust, and follow it. Regarding the distinct experiences you are about to learn, it's important to note that they are not listed in any particular order and you may not experience all of them. It's even common to experience different ones at different times, or all six of them during the same situation.

Intuition is literally a sixth sense—the ability to *sense* information. Intuition can also show up through the five physical senses, such as visual, auditory, and kinesthetic, and it can even use smell and taste to get your attention. As an intuition coach, I get impressions through all five physical senses and my sixth sense. I'm often given intuitive infor-mation in the sense my client responds to the most, or in the way that will be most effective to get their attention.

My client Alex is one example. Sadly, he had just been diagnosed with Hodgkin lymphoma. Alex was adamantly against allopathic medicine and leaned heavily toward alternative medicine. He had heard I was an intuition expert and wanted my guidance.

I could hardly believe my ears when Alex asked a most preposterous question. "Should I use my last $30,000 for a hair transplant or for lymphoma surgery?" The words were barely out of his mouth before an image flashed like lightning into my head, and no sooner had he stopped speaking when I blurted, "You're going to look great in your coffin with a full head of hair!" That shocked him right back into reality. He let out a chuckle about his foolish thinking and exclaimed, "What was I thinking?" I'm delighted to say Alex had that life-saving surgery and is alive and thriving with a full head of hair twenty years later.

Intuition knew the very image he needed to see and the message he needed to hear to save his life.

Let's explore how you can learn to do this for yourself. Read through the six ways to see which ones you connect with easily, and return to others that may require more practice.

DISTINCT EXPERIENCE OF URGE: THE NUDGE THAT GUIDES YOU

An Intuitive Urge has an unmistakable motivation to take a certain action or to avoid an action. You know *what* to do without knowing *why* you need to do it. An urge is recognized as heightened energy, often felt as a magnetic pull or a sudden inexplicable desire to do something specific such as make a phone call or buy turmeric, only to discover why later on when you need it for that new recipe.

Urge is not to be confused with a compulsive behavior, which is an action an individual engages in repeatedly—even when the individual wishes they could stop.

Many years ago, my friend Mary invited me to attend a networking meeting with her. I never enjoyed networking meetings and I didn't want to go. However, I kept getting the feeling I needed to go.

I was glad I went. I first ran into a long-lost friend, a wonderful treat in and of itself, but intuition had more in store for me. As I was walking back to my car, I heard a woman's voice yelling my name from across the parking lot. I looked up to see who it was. I didn't recognize her.

She made her way over to me, introduced herself, and enthusiastically shared what a profound impact my intuition book had on her life and career. She extended an invitation to speak at her conference for realtors a few months later, where I not only received fabulous new clients, but a new business mentor as well.

What opportunities might you be missing by not following the urges within you?

Remembering Your Urge Experience:
Common sensations or observations include
a high level of energy to act and clarity of direction.

REFLECTION:

Can you think of a time when you felt an unmistakable motivation to do something or a nudge to avoid something without knowing why? Close your eyes and relive the moment. What did it feel like? What happened as a result of honoring what you felt?

THE DISTINCT EXPERIENCE OF SNAPSHOT CLICK:
THE CONNECTING POINTS IN YOUR LIFE

A Snapshot Click is a moment of significance. It often stands out as though a photograph were taken. It might be something someone said or a particular line of lyrics to a song you find yourself singing. Whatever it might be, something about it stands out as though the subject has been highlighted.

Have you been carrying around an image of something you wish to experience some day? Did it possibly come to you in a dream? During a meditation? A recurring image you cannot even explain? Or a memory from the past that won't go away?

A Snapshot Click could be a single experience or many experiences woven together over time. It's as though they've been bookmarked and held for you to return to later. The click may come quickly or decades later. You may not know why it was bookmarked at the time it occurs. It's often forgotten until just the right moment, but when its significance is revealed you may think, *Now I know why that happened!* That's when it clicks into place.

Jack Canfield, co-author of the Chicken Soup for the Soul series, tells the story of how he and his co-author had been pulling out all the stops to make their book a best seller. It had been difficult to find someone to publish the book, but after submitting 144 proposals, they finally acquired a publisher. Now they needed to get the book to market. Little did Jack know that all of that hard work was about to pay off when he stopped in to purchase a drink at a local market one day and was drawn to a particular tabloid magazine. It was as if a camera had zoomed in on it.

At a conference the next day, a journalist from the very same magazine introduced herself, asking to interview him about his new book. Normally he may not have considered it, but based on his Snapshot Experience the day before at the local market, he agreed.

When his tabloid magazine interview hit the shelves, his book also hit the *New York Times* Bestseller list. Today there have been over 250

Chicken Soup for the Soul titles published, selling more than 500 million copies worldwide.

It pays to pay attention to your intuition! Been having a recurring image? Pay attention! Your intuition may be trying to get your attention.

Finding Your Snapshot-Click Experience:
Common sensations or observations include a
high level of presence, awareness, focused attention, and
absence of mental dividedness or resistance.

REFLECTION:

Locating the Snapshot

Bring to mind a memory of something that stands out to you. Write down the specific significant details. For example, Mary had been pressing her boyfriend for a marriage proposal. One day, after many exhausting arguments, she found herself gleefully and spontaneously singing, "I've got spurs that jingle, jangle, jingle. Oh, ain't you glad you're single."

Locating the Click

Using the Snapshot you identified, determine what your click is—that moment when you understood the significance of what happened. In Mary's case, the click happened when she observed how happy she felt while singing that line and realized she really didn't want to get married. She just wanted family and friends to stop putting demands on how she lived her life.

continued

Locating the Message

What is your intuition telling you? Please don't censor, analyze, or criticize what comes up and out of your heart. Write what bubbles up, even if you think it's your imagination.

THE DISTINCT EXPERIENCE OF WONDERMENT: THE PRESENCE OF AWE

There are two types of Wonderment, or what I like to call *Wondering*—Spontaneous Wondering and Deliberate Wondering.

Spontaneous Wondering is when you find yourself spontaneously wondering about a person, place, or thing with no intention of actually seeking an answer. It's just a lighthearted thought you happen to notice. Deliberate Wondering is intentionally used when you need an answer or solution but don't know how to proceed.

Whether you experience Spontaneous or Deliberate Wondering, it's important to pay attention to what shows up in your reality, and you do that by *noticing what you notice.*

I was redoing my office and needed a Parsons table to coordinate with one I had bought twenty-five years earlier but didn't know if that was even possible. All I did was "deliberately wonder" if I might be able to find one and didn't think about it anymore.

One day, I was driving to see a friend and noticed a store I hadn't seen before. I wondered if they might have a Parsons table. I tried to dismiss the idea since I was busy, but before I knew it, my car was doing a U-turn and I found myself walking through the front doors. Among an enormous sea of furniture, my eyes landed on exactly what I was looking for. A perfect Parsons table! I purchased it and was in and out in under ten minutes. I was in awe!

On another occasion, I opened the refrigerator drawer one day only to discover my newly purchased tomatoes were already going bad, *again*. I spontaneously wondered why they always went bad so fast. A few minutes later I turned on the television just in time to hear a famous chef say, "Never, ever put your tomatoes in the refrigerator with apples because apples emit a gas that ruins them!" Problem solved!

Finding Your Wonderment Experience:
Common sensations or observations include
wonder and awe, certainty and sureness,
lightheartedness, curiosity, astonishment, and detachment.

REFLECTION:

- Can you think of a time when you spontaneously wondered about someone and you ran into them? Or, what about a time you were worried about how something would turn out and you ended up astounded by the outcome?

- How or what did you feel when it happened? Did you dismiss the occurrence as coincidence or contemplate it?

THE DISTINCT EXPERIENCE OF KNOWING:
THE RESONANCE OF TRUTH

An Intuitive Knowing is distinct from understanding something based upon prior experience, such as in to how to make banana bread or solving a difficult math problem. Intuitive Knowing hasn't been previously known or experienced, yet it's something you know, deep within, without knowing how you know. Its sensations are undeniable and usually won't go away until acknowledged and acted on.

Sue woke up with a bad feeling in the pit of her stomach the morning of September 11, 2001. She was scheduled for an important meeting at the World Trade Center in New York City later that morning but had a very strong sense that she shouldn't go to work that day and called in sick. Her life was spared as a result.

Martha told me she *knew* her husband was having an affair, but, when questioned, he always denied it. She kept pressing for the truth because his words didn't resonate as true in her body. He finally admitted to the affair.

Truth resonates. Trust it!

Finding Your Knowing Experience:
Common sensations or observations include
certainty and resonance.

REFLECTION:

Recall a time you knew something without knowing how you knew it. Where did you feel the knowing—was it inside or outside your body? Was it subtle or strong? Did you act on your knowing? What was the result?

THE DISTINCT EXPERIENCE OF INSPIRATION: THE ENERGY OF CREATION

Inspiration is the experience of intense energy to create or act on something.

Can you think back to a time when you were truly inspired? You may have noticed a jolt of energy that immediately followed. Many people report that *inspiration always comes with the energy to make something happen*, whether it's to organize the garage, put a fundraiser together for a heartfelt cause, or to write your next novel.

My friend Josephine phoned me early one morning to tell me about a workshop she had attended the night before. She knew I had been struggling with depression since the birth of my son and was desperate to get my life together. "The leader is hosting another event next week," she said. "You have to go! It's what you're looking for to change your life!"

She had my attention! Just the thought of going to that workshop made me feel joy and a sense of hope.

Right up to the event I kept having a *feeling* that something great was about to happen. And my friend was right. The workshop was the key to changing my life. It may be hard to believe, but I walked out of the event knowing exactly what I was put on this earth to do. I found my life purpose and I've been living it for the past thirty years. If I had ignored all of the energy I felt about attending the workshop, you probably wouldn't be reading these words right now.

When the energy of inspiration arrives, you *must* act on it. Decide right now to choose inspiration over fear and doubt. Decide right now to honor the voice of inspiration, one of the most powerful ways intuition speaks to you!

Finding Your Inspiration Experience:
Common sensations or observations include
high energy, joy, bliss, and expansiveness.

REFLECTION:

Mentally relive a time you felt inspired. What did you do with that energy? Did you create something? What stimulated that inspiration? How did it feel? What stood out about that experience?

THE DISTINCT EXPERIENCE OF NO TIME: ALTERED TIME AND SPACE, THE HERE AND NOW

The Experience of No Time often occurs during urgent situations. It can even be created by the deliberate focus of attention. A significant event, be it painful or pleasurable, can automatically trigger the phenomenon that no time is passing. During a significant event, time may appear to slow down or speed up, and space may seem to expand or contract. It's normal for time and space to appear altered simultaneously.

To give you an idea of No Time, can you recall a memory or experience of being so engrossed in a task or conversation that you were totally flabbergasted to discover three hours had zipped right by? Did you marvel at where the time went?

Truly remarkable things happen with that kind of focus. What once may have taken several hours to complete might take only minutes. You're in the zone, as they say.

I've never met a person who couldn't recognize their intuition when they were fully present. If you bring your full focus to anything, your ability to communicate with intuition skyrockets.

In a No-Time phenomenon, such as an emergency, time can appear as though it has come to a screeching halt, yet everything is happening in mere seconds. One woman reported that as the airborne truck was about to crash down upon her, the truck appeared to be in slow motion as she quickly tucked herself under the steering wheel.

In any situation, when you command all of your focus on the here and now, you will find that you know exactly what you need to know, or do, without consciously having to figure anything out.

Finding Your No-Time Experience:
Common sensations or observations include expansion
and openness, presence, absence of time, peace, flow.

REFLECTION:

Remember a time in your life when you totally lost track of time. What were you doing? Who were you with? Were you inside or outside? Did you feel expanded or contracted? What was your perception of time or space?

FAITH IN INTUITION

Now that you know the Six Distinct Ways intuition speaks, it's time to apply them in your life.

Becoming good at anything requires practice. An effective way of learning to recognize the subtle nuances of intuition is to keep a journal or log of your daily experiences, including what you felt or sensed, the action you did or didn't take, and the final result. In as little as thirty days, patterns will emerge, making it easy to recognize when something is a True Intuition from when it isn't. Once you know how intuition best communicates with you, it will be hard to miss.

Trust isn't automatic. Just like with people, trusting your intuition is established over time through experience. By logging your experiences for thirty days you will create a body of evidence proving to yourself that intuition is indeed real and worthy of your trust. You'll soon marvel at how you navigate stressful situations with greater grace and ease. As you embark on the next thirty days, think of yourself as a scientist in an intuition laboratory researching and logging data. Be sure to take a lighthearted approach, as though you're going on an exciting adventure. Seriousness is like glue, making the entire process difficult.

In wrapping up Trusting Your Intuition, I leave you with the words of the late Mary Kay Ash, founder of Mary Kay Cosmetics and a true advocate for women.

> *I can't explain it analytically, but when the feeling is deep inside me, I know the right thing to do. I've talked about this sense with many women who say that although they can't explain it either, they've learned to trust it.*
>
> *Over the course of my career, I have worked with thousands and thousands of women. An objective observer would have predicted failure for a number of those who ended up succeeding. Relying on their instincts, they saw a path where no path had been charted, and they had the faith to take it. Their stories reaffirm my belief in woman's intuition that has helped me so much.*

> http://blog.marykayfoundation.org/corporate/archive/2017/08/21/
> mary-kay-ash-on-intuition.aspx

You have now been given six ways to recognize, follow, and utilize your intuition to leverage your life. May you cultivate the faith to trust and follow it. And may you lead with power, purpose, and certainty.

REFLECTION:

What concerns do you have about trusting and following intuition?

What causes you to doubt (not act upon) your intuition?

What might be the cost of not following your intuition?

What might be the benefits to you of trust and acting upon it?

What causes you to trust (act upon) your intuition?

CHAPTER 8

GROUP TRUST

A team is not a group of people who work together.
It is a group of people who trust each other.

~ Simon Sinek

I n the previous chapters on trust, we discussed trusting ourselves and trusting others. This chapter focuses on group or team trust. There is some overlap and familiarity and there are also nuances specific to team trust. In my long career, I have had many great teams; and there are some that stand out.

For the majority of my work life, I did not have the benefit of the framework described in this chapter. Yet as I look back, I can see that these elements were always in place for those standout teams. Since learning this framework, I strive to ensure these group-trust elements are always in place.

Though you may think specifically about work teams as you encounter various concepts in this chapter, you may also find this information useful in thinking about other groups of which you are a part—families, religious congregations, book clubs, philanthropic groups, and so on. This content is based largely on the research and work of Sue Hammond.

When I speak of team trust, I am speaking of the collection and interaction of all relationships in a team or a group. The team model has six dimensions that help create a team environment where members feel confident to be open with one another and take interpersonal risks. This is the graphic depiction of the framework for group trust. I often refer to it as the flower-petal model.

This framework, originally by Sue Hammond, is now the intellectual property of the ELI Group.

Let's review each of the six dimensions. The first is **Spirit of Unity**. This dimension reflects that we are not a collection of individuals; rather, we are a group that thinks and operates as one. We make decisions and generate ideas together in support of a shared vision. Each person in the group feels a sense of belonging. Every group member cares about the other group members and also feels cared about and for by the other group members. Each member has a commitment to one another and to the larger purpose or objective of the group. The group creates a positive environment. Each member contributes to that positive environment, one of optimism, clarity, and caring.

The second dimension is **Strategic Competence**. This is the general belief that the team has the skills to meet their goals and responsibilities. No single person has all the skills, but collectively, the group does. Each member of the group acknowledges, respects, defers to, and learns from the other members, thus increasing the capabilities of the group. Strategic Competence includes skillful decision-making, a commitment to innovation, reasoned risk-taking, and the ability to learn as a team.

The third dimension is **Predictability and Reliability**. Every member of the group relies on each of the other members to deliver on their commitments. Each member can count on other members of the team to do relevant and timely research, make business-driven recommendations, and deliver on time, within budget again and again. And if something happens that prevents a team member from doing these things, you can also reliably count on them to let everyone know and even ask for help. High-trust teams proactively communicate expectations to ensure each person on the team knows their roles and responsibilities, their performance objectives and metrics, and expectations of one another. These are mutual expectations. They are developed, communicated, and aligned to ensure understanding.

The fourth dimension is **Integrity and Openness**. This framework defines integrity as a commitment to take action for the greater good. You don't have a personal agenda. You don't have a hidden agenda. Openness is transparency. Others know what you're thinking because you share your objectives, your assumptions, your knowledge and experience, your concerns, your hopes, and your commitment. No one on the team has to guess. Such transparency reduces the risk of misunderstandings or breakdowns.

Integrity and openness also reflect the congruence of doing what you say you're going to do. You are "walking the talk." One of my dear friends and colleagues, Tracy Brown, likes to say, "You can't talk your way out of what you've walked your way into." You don't have to assume, interrogate, doubt, or worry about your team member following through. Another important aspect of this dimension is about giving credit to your team members for their individual results. It could also mean sharing credit with another team member if they've helped you achieve specific results. Remember, we're all in this together.

The fifth dimension is **Collaborative Intent**. Many of the skills necessary to achieve a collaborative team revolve around the ability to be open to other team members' points of view through constructive conversations. Constructive communication has an underlying intent to build mutual understanding. You have a point of view or perspective you want to share with the group *and* you are open to hearing and considering each team member's point of view or perspective as well. After the most effective constructive conversations, each team member leaves the conversation with a broader perspective and a deeper understanding of the topic being discussed. Whatever the topic or focus of our interaction, we cover the important focus areas regarding how our team supports the greater organizational goals. (We will discuss collaboration in further detail in chapter 9.)

The last dimension is **Psychological Safety**. This is at the center of the flower petals and touches each of the other five dimensions. It is both a foundational element of each of the other dimensions as well as an enhancer of each of these dimensions. It represents the environment created by the team that makes group members feel safe enough to be vulnerable and take interpersonal risks with one another in order to achieve goals. You know that you can ask questions and not fear ridicule or shame. You can offer a different point of view or perspective without fear of resistance or rejection. You can speak your truth, period. Your contributions will be invited, acknowledged, and considered in the process of the group arriving at a decision or delivering desired results.

ACTIVITY:

Use a scale of 1–5 (1 = Low, 5 = High)

Dimension	My Team	My Boss's Team
Spirit of Unity		
Strategic Competence		
Predictability & Reliability		
Integrity & Openness		
Collaborative Intent		
Psychological Safety		
Total		

Using a scale of 1 to 5 (1 = Low, 5 = High), how would you assess your team against these six dimensions? Record your assessment numbers in the preceding table. Total your scores. (Possible total scores are 6 to 30.) Now do the same thing for your boss's team, of which you are a member, and total those scores. How do the two scores compare? The same score? One is lower or higher than the other? Any surprises or insights?

In my experience doing this activity with many teams over several years, program participants often rate their own teams higher than their boss's team. It doesn't happen every time, but it occurs with great regularity. If you came to this conclusion with your assessment, I want to challenge your assumptions. Remember, one of the most common ways to derail effective leadership is thinking you're showing up one way when, in actuality, the world is seeing and experiencing you very differently. The same thing can be seen when completing this activity. You believe your team has a great spirit of unity, integrity and openness, psychological safety, and so on. And yet, you also want to check to see if your team feels the same way you do.

Before you decide to give your team this chart and ask them to assess the team, I recommend you have a conversation with them to discuss examples and share stories that reflect each dimension. How would you describe Spirit of Unity? How would you describe the shared vision? When have you all done a good job of *collaborating*? What is an example of when you all didn't collaborate very effectively? Can you think of a time when you were afraid to speak up? What do you think prevented you from speaking up? What would need to happen for you to speak up more in the future?

By having this kind of conversation, you are building group trust through describing what each of these six dimensions looks like when the system is working well and also when it isn't. It is an actionable way to arrive at higher group trust. Remember, you can't undo the past, so I recommend you don't dwell on it. Spend your collective intellectual horsepower getting really clear about how each member would define group trust going forward. You are now ready to do a baseline assessment. Where do you all think you are today?

Whatever that assessment might be, you can lead your team through a process of actionable items that will help you achieve higher group trust and the strong relationships and outstanding results that come with that high trust. You can do another assessment three to six months later to determine whether and what improvements have occurred. Ensure that each team member has a responsibility in creating this high-trust team environment.

REFLECTION:

Consider these questions for both the team you lead and as a member of your boss's team.

How would you rate your team's level (or degree) of group trust?

What are you doing to contribute to high team trust?

What are you doing that might undermine high team trust?

What can you do differently, moving forward?

What can you do differently in your boss's team going forward to build higher team trust?

You can likely think of teams you've been on that had high trust as well as those that didn't. My personal experience is that the best teams are rare, and we may not always appreciate them in the moment. What I have found is that, if I focus on these six dimensions, the probability is much higher that my current team can be one of high trust with a sense of caring and psychological safety.

CHAPTER 9

MANAGING CONFLICT AND ENRICHING RELATIONSHIPS

One may be of a different opinion and still be my friend.

~ Margaret Cavendish

I sometimes get calls from potential clients asking me to come and teach a workshop to eliminate conflicts in their organization. I laugh and reply, "I want to know about that workshop!" What I teach is about managing conflict, which involves working through a conflict effectively. I also want to help people maintain relationships when their counterpart is on the other side of an issue.

The reality is that having conflicts in our lives is inevitable. Each of us brings our life experiences, beliefs, values, and points of view to every conversation. Because those experiences, beliefs, and values vary widely, the probability is high that we will live and work with people whose ideas and approaches will be different from ours. Conflict occurs most often when it is time to make a decision. The first question, which naturally and instantaneously arises, is: "Are we going to do it your way or my way?" The idea here is to figure out how to move through those decision-making and conflict situations with intentionality and effectiveness. My life experience is that the more we have to talk about it and disagree again and again, the more I am putting my relationship with you at risk. So let's get smarter and develop some strategies for moving more intentionally and competently through conflict conversations.

The information I'm sharing with you is based on the work of Kenneth Thomas and Ralph Kilmann, also referred to as the "Thomas-Kilmann model." They have also developed an assessment tool that analyzes our typical reactions to different conflict scenarios. I have found their work to be very helpful in knowing more about my options and when to use each of their five conflict response modes. Let's look at their model at the macro level.

As with many consultants, the Thomas-Kilmann model relies on two axes. The vertical axis represents an assertiveness scale. I refer to this axis as the Results scale. The horizontal axis represents the cooperativeness scale. I refer to this axis as the Relationship scale.

There are five conflict response modes. Here is how you can connect the axes scales and the conflict response modes.

POSSIBLE RESPONSES TO CONFLICT

Conflict Response Mode	Results	Relationships
Avoiding	Low	Low
Accommodating	Low	High
Competing	High	Low
Collaborating	High	High
Compromising	Medium	Medium

Now let's look at each of these conflict response modes individually. Please note that I will be using some terms interchangeably, not to confuse you but rather to encourage you to think about each of the response modes as tools in your tool kit or as strategies for achieving your desired outcomes. Keep in mind, there is no "right answer" in how frequently I use any one of these response modes at any given time. The goal is to know "what tool to use when" and to feel competent and confident in my abilities to use each one. Let's review each of the five response modes—in what situation you would use each one, what skills are required to be competent, and what is likely to happen if you overuse or underuse any one of them.

For each of the five conflict response modes, I will share a framework to better understand each mode. First, I will offer a tagline to think about or relate to a specific conflict mode. Second, I'll review situations or scenarios in which you would use a particular conflict mode. Third, I'll offer the skills to be developed in order to effectively display the conflict mode. Fourth, I'll provide possible consequences in the overuse or underuse of each particular conflict mode.

AVOIDING

Some people tell me they think it is never wise to avoid a conflict. I beg to differ. *Avoiding* is an effective strategy when used in the right situation—I see *avoiding* as another way of "choosing your battles." It can also be used as a short-term and/or a long-term strategy for managing conflicts.

	Tagline	"I'll think about it tomorrow"
Avoiding	**Situation**	• Reducing tensions • Buying time • Staying out of the middle
	Skills	• Ability to withdraw • Sidestepping • Sense of timing • Ability to leave things unresolved
	Overuse	• Lack of influence • Decisions made by default • Issues fester/cautious climate • Lack of prioritization • Lack of delegation • Work overload
	Underuse	• Hostility/Hurt feelings

The tagline here is: "I'll think about it tomorrow." Maybe the issue is too overwhelming to tackle right now. Maybe you're not prepared because you haven't done your homework. Maybe you are not clear about your own position on a particular issue. Whatever the case, you are pulling out of or delaying the conversation necessary to resolve the conflict.

SITUATIONS RELATED TO AVOIDING

If you are going to practice and become proficient at knowing what tool to use when, you will need to anticipate and get clear about the nature of the interaction and your objectives. When you find yourself in one of the following situations, you might want to open up your tool kit and use your *avoiding* tool. Let's talk about each of these situations.

• **Reducing Tensions** – Have you ever been in one of those conversations when voices are getting louder, fists are pounding the table, and faces are getting red? If you haven't been involved in one of those, good for you. But maybe you've observed such an interaction. These are often referred to as "escalating situations," where tensions are clearly rising. We can use a short-term or temporary *avoid* approach to de-escalate the situation. I want to link this to the next situation: "Buying Time."

- **Buying Time** – This represents those times when you want to delay the conversation until you have time to do additional research, have additional conversations, or think about the issue further. At that point, you can determine which of the five response modes is the most appropriate to move forward in your next conversation.

- **Staying Out of the Middle** – You want to allow others to handle the conflicts that are theirs to resolve. The best way to describe this situation is reflected in the example below.

  ○ **Example:** Employee A comes to you and says he or she can't work with Employee B. Your recommended leadership approach or response:

  ○ **Listen** and probe for clarification. Do not blame or embarrass.

  ○ **Ask** Employee A what a good relationship would look like going forward. Don't be surprised if they struggle answering or take a self-serving or biased view. Coach them regarding mutuality and realistic expectations. This is about clarity.

  ○ **Ask** Employee A what they have done to create the kind of relationship they've described going forward. This is about responsibility.

  ○ **State** your expectations. For example, no workplace distractions or loss of productivity, as well as your expectation that Employee A will have a conversation with Employee B to resolve the issue. This is about setting and aligning expectations.

  ○ **Practice** the conversation with Employee A, assuming the role of Employee B. Provide coaching for greater effectiveness and building capacity for self-sufficiency going forward in resolving difficult situations. This is about creating capacity.

○ **State** that you will check back to see how the conversation went, stressing what Employee A learned going through the process. *Note*: Don't be surprised if the conversation doesn't occur. Follow up. This is about accountability.

○ If it does occur, ask the three learning agility questions: 1) What did you do? 2) What did you learn? and 3) How will it help you going forward?

○ If the conversation doesn't occur, coach around priorities, perspective, courage, and accountability.

Thoughts to consider:

○ If you solve the issue for the employee, your reward is that they will continue to bring you all their problems to solve. That is not the best use of your time, energy, and focus.

○ If you attempt to solve it but are unsuccessful, they blame you and it is **not** your conflict.

SKILLS RELATED TO AVOIDING

• **Ability to Withdraw** – It is okay to start withdrawing from any given situation. This can be a short-term or long-term solution. Withdrawing is an opportunity to pull away from a given situation. You must be willing to not engage in a conflict conversation, and your inclination or default pattern to want to engage have to be fought against. Withdrawing means merely that you are choosing not to be a part of a conversation because you want to avoid a particular conflict.

- **Sidestepping** – This skill is one that reflects your ability to tactfully avoid a conflict conversation. Language of sidestepping would include, "This is not a conversation that I choose to be engaged in." Another example of sidestepping language would be, "I don't believe I have anything to offer in this conversation."

- **Sense of Timing** – When you find yourself in conversations where tensions are rising, you must know when to de-escalate or to let a perhaps heated and uncomfortable situation continue. When you find that another person is losing their temper, being disrespectful, or making threats, you clearly want to de-escalate quickly. To have a sense of timing is to know when to let them escalate and when you want to de-escalate. In most situations, de-escalation is preferable. This is when you want to remove yourself and get clearer about how you want to reengage in the conversation.

  On rare occasions, conversations escalate to the point of being a breakdown. One thing I often share in my training is that sometimes a breakdown must take place before a breakthrough can manifest. These instances are rare and yet powerful. Let me give you an analogy. When you break your arm and it is set properly, the bone in your arm where the break occurred is stronger after you've broken it than it was before you broke it. We measure this by reviewing the X-ray that shows the density of the bone is stronger after the break has occurred and mended. This is much like our relationships. If our relationship can withstand division or being on two sides of a particular issue, and we can work through that situation, then our relationship is stronger because we know it can withstand such differences.

  One of my colleagues Mia Mbroh recently extended this analogy . . . And when your arm is in that cast, you feel uncomfortable. In addition, you have to give your arm (and your relationship) time to heal.

I recall the Margaret Cavendish quote at the beginning of this chapter: "One can be of a different opinion and still be my friend." We can have a break and still be friends. In fact, our friendship will be stronger because we had a difference of opinion and worked through it. That continued friendship is in fact the equivalent of a breakthrough in the phrase "there sometimes has to be a breakdown before a breakthrough can manifest."

- **Ability to Leave Things Unresolved** – This particular skill is difficult to achieve. Our brains are a closed-looped system. Once we get a thought into our brains, it will keep cycling or churning in our heads until it gets resolved. To get resolved is to close the loop. We know this to be true because these swirling thoughts often keep us awake at night, because we feel like something is undone.

  Keep notepads on your bedside table? How many of us set alarms on our phones to ensure that we don't forget something? These are two simple examples of how we find a temporary place to put our swirling thoughts so we can get the rest that we need. Use your own methods to allow your brain to find a temporary place for your swirling thoughts. You can buy yourself time to resolve the issue at a more strategic or appropriate time based on your overall strategy for managing a particular complex situation.

OVERUSE OF AVOIDING

You may have heard the saying that any strength taken to an extreme can become a weakness. That is the case if we overuse any one conflict response mode no matter what the situation might call for. If I overuse *avoiding*, making it my go-to strategy, here are some **potential consequences**:

- **Lack of Influence** – If you have a tendency or default to avoid when it comes to speaking your opinion or sharing your point of view, you have very limited influence on outcomes. Your input is lost.

- **Decisions Made by Default** – Have you ever been in a meeting or on a call when the person running the session provides direction or a recommendation and then asks for input? No one says a word when given the opportunity. Then they walk out of the meeting and may or may not follow the direction given. Maybe that silent person was you. Maybe it was a colleague. The choice to remain silent on a matter but then not behave as agreed to is a form of passive-aggressive behavior. Being passive in the meeting and not executing as directed or requested can be seen as aggressive insubordination at its worst, or as not being a trustworthy or effective leader. Passive-aggressive behavior is *not* leadership behavior.

Let me offer some tips for you if you find yourself in this situation:

  - ○ If you know what topics or decisions are going to be reviewed in a meeting, be prepared. That means you have done your homework, developed a clear point of view, prepared your case or reasoning, and maybe even had some "meetings before the meeting." If so, you can speak up with clarity and confidence.

  - ○ You can have a quick follow-up call or meeting with the leader to voice your concerns or point of view privately. This is an after-the-fact approach and may or may not result in you feeling heard or having influence.

  - ○ If it is a colleague that privately shares with you that they will not be following the direction of the meeting leader, you still have an opportunity to take a leadership stance. You might say to them, "It sounds like you feel strongly that the direction offered is not the most effective approach. I recommend you talk to the meeting leader and let them know how you feel." This way, you are providing a leadership point of view that builds trust *and* allows you to stay out of the middle. It is not your job to go "tattle" on your colleague (unless, of course, their solution involves an illegal or dangerous approach, in which case, you let them know you are not on board).

- **Issues Fester/Cautious Climate** – When I think of this situation, I often think about exchanged glances or the "elephant in the room." We all know an uncomfortable or unpleasant issue is circulating, but no one wants to be the person to bring it up. We keep hoping someone else will bring it up, or, better yet, it will just go away. In my experience, it rarely does, and it usually surfaces at the most inopportune times. In the meantime, the continued avoidance of the undiscussable creates a cautious climate that is not conducive to doing our best or most productive work.

- **Work Overload** – If your boss or client asks you to do something and your answer is always yes, you are likely to find yourself in a work overload position. This is an example of overusing *avoiding* in order to minimize conflict. You may remember that we talked about this in chapter 6, Setting and Maintaining Boundaries. Work overload often results in working more hours than you can truly afford in your pursuit of work-life balance.

- **Lack of Prioritization** – If you don't prioritize, everything becomes a priority. When I've coached women around saying no or asking for reprioritization, and the women try this new behavior, they are amazed to receive no pushback or retribution as they feared would happen if and when they said no. I coach everyone, both men and women, to always have their list of priorities with them wherever they go. Let's imagine that you're walking down the hall and your boss stops you and asks you to work on a project. Your next step would be to pull out your priority list and say, "Based on the commitments I've already made and the assignments you've already given to me, where does this project fit from a priority standpoint?" Your boss now has the option of evaluating your already committed project list and saying something like, "You know, it looks like you already have a full plate. Let me ask someone else to do this project."

Another option might be that the boss or whoever the requester is says, "We need to get it done by a certain date." If that's the case, you would then ask for relief on the deliverables of some of your other projects that you've already committed to and that have already been prioritized.

Let's say that you have ten items on your prioritized list. Your boss has now given you a new number-one priority. Your request is to ask if you can push or delay any deliverable dates on your other projects, now prioritized items number two through eleven. Again, there are two potential options: 1) Your boss says, "Yes" or your boss says, "Yes, bring me the adjustments in deliverables that would be required in order for you to make this your number-one priority."

A second option is the boss says "no" or says, "No, we need to get all of them done as committed." My coaching to you, should this be the option that plays out, is to ensure that the boss knows what the effort is that will be required in order to meet commitments as noted. In other words, you might say, "Okay, boss, I understand the need to get it all done. I want you to know that we will likely have to work overtime and potentially weekends to get all of these projects done in their committed timelines. Are you okay with that?" The teaching point here goes back to one of our Foundational Elements: *Results + Recognition = Power/ Influence*. You want to ensure that your considerable effort is recognized so that you get credit for not only achieving the results but also the recognition of the hard work, above and beyond the performance required to deliver on all prioritized commitments.

- **Lack of Delegation** – You are wary of delegating items to your team because you fear their pushback based on that they already have a significant amount of work to do. Therefore, you avoid delegating to your team in order to avoid the conflict or a difficult conversation. I know that as a leader of the many teams I've led over the years, I worked hard to delegate tasks that would in fact develop my direct reports and help them achieve their career objectives. Avoiding conflict results in not only more work on your plate, but less learning for others. I also advised my direct reports that I would continue delegating such tasks to them until they told me that they couldn't take any more on, and to meet the commitments that they already made based on previously assigned projects or tasks. In other words, I would keep giving them work until they said, "No more."

When I delegated tasks that I simply didn't want to do, my direct employees could see through that . . . and, yes, this could have potentially resulted in conflict. I'm not recommending that you delegate unpleasant tasks or ones you don't want to do. I am suggesting that you delegate tasks, projects, and assignments for purposes of developing your direct reports with the specific objective that it is their job to complete these kinds of tasks. Women often find it "easier" to accept incomplete or lesser quality work and finish it than to hold the other person accountable for an acceptable level of performance. Also, women tend to be more willing to inconvenience themselves by not delegating and taking on more work themselves rather than inconveniencing another person. Watch out for these tendencies if my description fits your default patterns.

UNDERUSE OF AVOIDING

- **Hostility/Hurt Feelings** – The drawback associated with an underuse of *avoiding* is that it can create a relationship that includes hostility and hurt feelings. The point here is that if you think every conflict situation has to be addressed or resolved—and done so immediately—that would constitute an underuse of *avoiding*. If you are always wanting to have a conflict conversation, you may be seen as a bully, a person who always has to win, and even a poor team player. That's not the definition of leadership. We want to be mindful about the appropriate use of *avoiding*.

REFLECTION:

Think of a time when you have avoided a conflict.

Was avoiding an effective strategy?

Do you have a situation where you are currently avoiding a conflict?

Is that a strategic choice or a default response?

ACCOMMODATING

Now we are going to talk about the conflict response mode of *accommodating*—this response is most appropriate when the relationship is more important than the result. The tagline for *accommodating* is: "It would be my pleasure." I always imagine doing a little curtsy as I utter these words. The tagline represents the sentiment that you will fully accept the position, decision, or recommendation of another person. There is no pushback, no second-guessing.

	Tagline	"It would be my pleasure"
Accommodating	**Situation**	• Showing reasonableness/Creating goodwill • Developing performance • Retreating/Giving in
	Skills	• Selflessness • Obeying orders • Ability to yield
	Overuse	• Ideas get little action/ Restricted influence • Loss of contribution • Anarchy
	Underuse	• Lack of rapport • Low morale • Seen as unyielding • Seen as a poor team player

ACCOMMODATING SITUATIONS

Now we'll discuss those situations where *accommodating* is the right tool to use.

- **Showing Reasonableness/Creating Goodwill** – Showing reasonableness and creating goodwill go hand in hand. Let's say that you and I are starting a new relationship and we want to get it off on the right track. If the outcome is less important to me than building a strong relationship with you, then that would be an appropriate use of *accommodating*. We will do it your way and I can let my way go.

- **Developing Performance** – Here are the two scenarios in which the developing performance takes shape. The first—I have specifically gone out and hired someone or brought someone in from outside my organization because I want a fresh perspective. The research shows that this is a common occurrence in the hiring process; however, once that person is hired and offering new thoughts, ideas, and recommendations, we often shut them down with comments like, "That wouldn't work" or "We've tried that before." This is like beating their head against the wall, and results in them not feeling valued or not being able to bring all their knowledge, experience, and perspective to the table or to their job. Either the company asks them to leave because the person is not considered a "good fit" or the person resigns because they are not able to bring the best of themselves to the role. To allow that person to bring in and apply their fresh thinking is to accommodate them. It helps you achieve your objective of fresh thinking.

The second example of developing performance comes in the form of hiring new people early in their careers. In today's world we might think of millennials as falling into this category. We also know that millennials can get a bad name for being the "entitled" generation. They want it all, they want it now, and they don't understand how the world works. This thinking serves no one. Tapping into the perspective of the knowledge, the skills, and the education that this younger workforce has would encourage us to ponder how things could be done differently. Consider their skills and abilities in the use of technology. Most organizations that I work with are looking for innovation and productivity gains on a regular and continuous basis.

Offering a young employee a challenge or opportunity—perhaps something low risk, low visibility, and supervised—enables you to benefit from more current technology or processes. Perhaps what the younger employee has to offer is wonderful. Their skills meet needs in a more effective and productive way. It's a learning opportunity for that younger employee, which again serves everyone in the long run, especially when you ensure that the employee understands what worked, what didn't work, and what they may want to do going forward. Encouraging a young person to introduce new ideas and to apply them is an example of *accommodating*, rather than resisting change or stereotyping young people.

- **Retreating/Giving In** – The last situation in which you would use *accommodating* is in retreating or giving in. This is when you've worked hard to implement what you thought would be a good solution but it didn't work. You can think of this as using the *accommodating* conflict response mode as a secondary approach. Your first approach may have been one of *competing* (which we'll cover later in this chapter). By *accommodating* in a retreating or giving-in scenario, you are showing humility and learning, attributes that build trust and reflect a willingness to incorporate new thinking and ideas, while also recognizing staff contributions toward effective and productive solutions.

ACCOMMODATING SKILLS

The skills required to be good at *accommodating* include:

- **Selflessness** – Selflessness is about foregoing your desires and being readily willing to do it another person's way. You value your relationships as more important than getting your way.

- **Obeying Orders** – Obeying orders often shows up in the hierarchy of positional power. Your boss asked you to do it this way. Your customer asked you to do it this way. A family member asked you to do it a certain way, and you choose to comply with their recommendation, idea, or solution.

- **Ability to Yield** – The last skill is the ability to yield. Think about driving in a city—whether it's yielding to someone entering the ramp on an interstate highway or at a four-way stop, or letting a car in front of you during heavy traffic. It can even be yielding that prize parking spot when you're trying to get in and out of a particular location. Our willingness and ability to yield in those situations is part of *accommodating* another's need or idea.

One of the things I've learned since teaching this material for the past twenty-plus years is that it is equally important to define what *accommodating* is not. It is not declaring, "We'll do it your way this time and my way the next time." That is scorekeeping. *Accommodating* is also not about begrudgingly doing it the other person's way, and when it doesn't work, saying, "I told you so." That is a more self-righteous attitude. It is not about doing it the other person's way and then undermining or sabotaging their approach to ensure it doesn't work. I see that as mean-spirited, and it certainly doesn't reflect a leadership mindset.

OVERUSE OF ACCOMMODATING

Now let's talk about the impact of overusing *accommodating*.

- **Ideas Get Little Action/Restricted Influence** – If you are always accommodating everyone else in their recommendations and solutions, then your ideas get little action because they're not implemented. Therefore, you have little or no influence in the organization because you're always doing it the other person's way.
- **Loss of Contribution** – Your best work and thinking is withheld. There is a loss of your contributions to the organization and you may even feel overlooked and unvalued.

- **Anarchy** – Generally speaking, leaders are trying to get the organization all marching in the same direction toward a shared goal or objective. When the leader is *accommodating* everyone else, and perhaps even encouraging a culture of accommodation, then getting everyone marching in the same direction is much more difficult. Think of it as, instead of all the arrows pointing in the same direction toward that goal or objective, the arrows are pointing in all kinds of directions and you have a culture of chaos and confusion. That's what I mean by anarchy.

UNDERUSE OF ACCOMMODATING

As with each of the conflict response modes, underuse can have unintended consequences regarding not only your desired outcomes but also your reputation as an effective leader.

- **Lack of Rapport** – If you never accommodate, building rapport with your peers, boss, team, and customers may be difficult for you. That lack of rapport impedes your ability to build strong relationships.

- **Low Morale** – If you don't build strong relationships, an environment or a culture of low morale will be the result.

- **Seen as Unyielding** – People will dread working with you if you are never willing to accommodate their thinking, their ideas. You may be seen as unyielding, which is a kind way of saying "stubborn." No matter what leadership literature you may research, stubborn will likely not show up as a desired leadership attribute.

- **Seen as a Poor Team Player** – You may also be seen as a poor team player because of the contentious relationships within your team or with your boss, customer(s), and colleagues. We all know that most work that needs to be accomplished today requires us to work as a strong team.

REFLECTION:

Think of a time when you have accommodated in a conflict.

Was accommodating an effective strategy?

Do you have a situation where you are currently accommodating in a conflict?

Is that a strategic choice or a default response?

COMPETING

The *competing* conflict mode often carries a negative connotation. People who have *competing* as a recurring default—think overuse—are often seen as always having to get their way or winning every time. I want to stress that *competing* is an effective tool in your tool kit when used with the right intentions and in the right situation. The *competing* conflict response is an effective strategy when I believe that my idea, position, or recommendation is the most effective or useful one—*in service to* the client, market, or organization. This is about intentions. If your solution is in service to something bigger, it is seen as effective. If it is seen as you pushing your own agenda for your own personal gain or benefit, it will likely be viewed negatively.

That leads to the tagline of: "My way or the highway." In other words, "I want what I want and I am not willing to consider any other alternatives." Typically, when I ask my program participants if they've ever worked for or with someone who reflected this tagline, many hands go up. Then, I ask them how many might say the same thing about themselves. A few hands usually go up accompanied by nervous laughter. Again, I caution you, it's the overuse you want to watch out for.

	Tagline	"My way or the highway"
Competing	**Situation**	• Taking quick action • Making unpopular decisions • Standing up for vital issues
	Skills	• Ability to argue or debate • Standing your ground • Stating your position clearly • Stating your facts • Differentiating between fact and opinion • Ability to use rank, positional power, or influence
	Overuse	• Lack of feedback • Reduced learning • Low empowerment • Surrounded by "yes" people
	Underuse	• Restricted influence • Seen as indecisive • Contributions are withheld

COMPETING SITUATIONS

Let's outline the circumstances when *competing* is the most effective tool to use.

- **Taking Quick Action** – As a leader, you are being asked to make decisions and take action all of the time, every day. What I'm talking about here are those decisions that require your immediate attention and action. Perhaps an employee on a manufacturing line has gotten hurt, or an irate customer is demanding to speak to the person in charge. You don't have to pull a task force together. You don't have to do any research. You drop whatever you are doing and take action. No questions asked.

- **Making Unpopular Decisions** – This situation is one of the more dreaded aspects of being a leader. You have to make a decision that won't please everyone. The fallout of some of these decisions can include requiring mandatory overtime, working weekends to meet a deadline, cutting the budget, or even restructuring resulting in loss of jobs. Rest assured, you've hopefully considered other alternatives or possibilities before arriving at your position. And, you have to move forward based on contractual commitments, regulatory or legal requirements, or even the ongoing future of the organization.

- **Standing Up for Vital Issues** – This is an important time to be clear about your values and principles. That is what I mean about vital issues. Do you stand up for what you believe in—integrity, mutual respect, ethical behavior? Do you accept responsibility for your and your team's work or results, rather than casting blame or taking credit for someone else's work? Do you "speak truth to power" even when the stakes are high? One of my favorite quotes from the movie *The Contender* is: "Principles are only principles when they are practiced when they are inconvenient." That is at the heart of standing up for vital issues.

COMPETING SKILLS

These are the skills necessary to be effective at *competing*.

- **Ability to Argue or Debate** – Often we see arguing as something to avoid. I suggest you reframe arguing into standing up for what you believe. We can't be afraid of engaging in conversations that matter. Do your homework, be clear about your position, know your facts, *and* be knowledgeable about any opposing views. In preparation for debates, debaters are often asked to represent the other side so that they are ready for whatever may come at them.

- **Standing Your Ground** – When you are in a *competing* conversation, the back-and-forth is plentiful. You will make your points and also listen carefully to the points made by the other person(s). In the best situations, you are prepared, and you will not be surprised by what the other person has to say. Even when the other person offers strong points, standing strong in your own position, having facts to support it, and stating them with confidence is what puts you in the best place to achieve your desired outcome. I often describe this as having the courage of your convictions.

- **Stating Your Position Clearly** – When you are stating your position, you need to be clear, crisp, and concise. Practice it, say it out loud, and share it with someone you trust who will give you constructive feedback on the clarity of your position. When you use too many words, ramble, or start repeating yourself, you will lose your audience and your credibility. You want to show up as credible and confident. Practicing out loud is most helpful. When you're under pressure, your thinking can get clouded. When you've practiced the words out loud several times, they will come to you more easily.

- **Stating Your Facts** – The strength of your position is only as strong as the facts on which you've based it. Ensure your sources are legitimate, relevant, and current. That doesn't mean that earlier research is not relevant. You also need to be prepared to hear refuting research. Research often does contradict. I had a boss who once told me I needed to "triangulate the data." That meant I needed to have three sources of data to support each fact I was touting. It requires more work on your part but will give you greater confidence when presenting and defending your position.

- **Differentiating between Fact and Opinion** – Let's be really clear: facts can be sourced, while opinions are a reflection of our thoughts and feelings based on our interpretation of facts. For instance, one of us may think the temperature of a room is too hot, another too cold, and another just right. These are opinions. The fact is that the thermostat is set at seventy-four degrees.

- **Ability to Use Rank, Positional Power, or Influence** – Think back to earlier chapters where we talked about power. We discussed positional, relational, and personal power. We also talked about Heim's work and how a feminine approach reflects a flat structure (relational power) and a masculine approach reflects a hierarchical structure (positional power). What I have learned in my forty-plus years of being in formal leadership roles is that my team is looking to me to be decisive (taking quick action), to make the tough calls (making unpopular decisions), and to fight for what I believe in (standing up for vital issues). It is my responsibility, and I hold myself accountable for fulfilling that responsibility.

By building these skills, and with preparation and practice, you will gain greater confidence using this *competing* approach. Personally, I never find this easy, *yet* I do find it very rewarding when I have success and believe I've done the right thing. Even when I don't get what I think is the "right" outcome, I still feel good because I fulfilled my responsibilities, acted in accordance with my values, and stood up for what I believed in. I often think, "I can get up the next morning, look myself in the mirror, and feel good as I start a new day."

OVERUSE OF COMPETING

A reminder, the overuse of *competing* is what gives *competing* a bad name, and can result in the following detrimental consequences:

- **Lack of Feedback** – If it always has to be your way, either because you always want to win or you are taking a self-serving position, those around you will eventually shut down. They will stop offering their own thoughts, ideas, recommendations, or perspectives because their words fall on deaf ears. Communication has become a one-way rather than a two-way conversation, with a healthy, validating exchange.

- **Reduced Learning** – If you are not receiving feedback, different views or perspectives, or people are not challenging you, your learning is reduced. You can learn so much by asking questions and inviting others' viewpoints, thereby broadening your own perspective and consideration for conclusions and decisions.

- **Low Empowerment** – When people offer ideas, share their points of view, or get creative with solutions and they are ignored or, worse yet, ridiculed, then pretty soon they just stop. If it goes in one ear and right out the other, then why bother. People often choose to just follow orders, creating a compliant culture when most organizations are seeking innovation. Or employees request transfers and may even start looking for a new job outside of the organization. High voluntary turnover is often a symptom of the overuse of *competing*.

- **Surrounded by "Yes" People** – If you shut those down around you and believe you *always* have the only right answer, you will soon be surrounded by people who tell you only what you want to hear. Perhaps it's to avoid your wrath or feed your ego, or to advance their career. A phrase I often hear is "they are living in an echo chamber." You never talk to people with diverse views because it means they don't agree with you. You can become very isolated when you only hear your thoughts and words being parroted back to you. You can also be labeled as naïve or narrow-minded. None of these labels are used to describe a strong leader.

UNDERUSE OF COMPETING

And just as *overuse* is a "watch out," so is *underuse*. The results can be:

- **Restricted Influence** – It is hard for you to wield influence if you are not willing to step up and speak up. You will always be following the direction of someone else.

- **Seen as Indecisive** – If you don't declare your position and almost always acquiesce to another, you will be seen as indecisive, wishy-washy, and having no courage regarding your position or conviction.

- **Contributions Are Withheld** – If you are following the lead of another, clearly you are not contributing your best thinking or your best work. And I have to admit, it makes me sad when every employee can't contribute the best of themselves.

Competing is a powerful tool in your tool kit!

REFLECTION:

Think of a time when you have used competing in a conflict.

How was competing an effective or ineffective strategy?

Do you have a situation where you are currently competing in a conflict?

Is that a strategic choice or a default response?

COLLABORATING

Collaborating is an effective approach when both the results and the relationship are important. We are living in a world of matrix organizations, dual reporting lines, and operating on a global basis. Knowing how to truly collaborate is an important leadership competency. To that end, let me describe what I mean regarding collaboration. The Oxford dictionary defines *collaboration* as "working jointly on an activity, especially to produce or create something."

And before we go too far, let me differentiate between *competing* and *collaborating*. In *competing*, I come to the table with a "one-hundred percent" position or answer. In *collaborating*, I come with a point of view, a perspective, functional knowledge, or research, and so does everyone else. No one of us has the complete or ideal answer. Rather, we are going to create it together. This is where brainstorming, generative thinking, and innovation occur. We walk away from our time together with a decision, answer, or solution that no one of us could have developed on our own.

If you are taking a collaborative approach, let others know that. And, more importantly, let them know what you mean by *collaborating*. You might send out a note to meeting participants prior to your gathering and tell them you will run the meeting as a collaboration. You would declare your expectations, including:

- Here is the decision we need to make or the problem we need to solve.

- Come prepared with your experience, research, ideas, and functional expertise, *and* (and this is really important) . . .

- Be prepared for others to bring their experience, research, ideas, and functional expertise.

- We will respectfully listen to one another and give serious weight and consideration to what everyone has to say.

- We will be creating the answer together. We will ask probing and clarifying questions.

- We will build on one another's ideas, taking the best that each of us has to offer.

You can see how the tagline of: "Two heads are better than one" applies. The *collaborating* approach respects the diversity of experience and ideas reflected in the people contributing in useful ways. Giving weight and consideration to everyone's thoughts and ideas is an act of inclusion.

	Tagline	"Two heads are better than one"
Collaborating	**Situation**	• Merging perspectives/Integrating ideas • Learning • Gaining commitment
	Skills	• Ability to listen • Nonthreatening confrontation • Analyzing input/Identifying concerns • Facilitating
	Overuse	• Too much time on trivial matters/ Work overload • Diffused responsibility • Others may take advantage
	Underuse	• Loss of mutual gains • Low empowerment/Lack of commitment • Loss of innovation

COLLABORATING SITUATIONS

I find that we often see collaboration as a positive strategy. It certainly plays to relational power and a flat structure. And, it is useful when used in the right situations.

- **Merging Perspectives/Integrating Ideas** – As I have described previously, the very definition of collaboration is about merging perspectives, and valuing and embracing the diversity of thought. Once ideas are out on the table, you begin to integrate them into a coherent new solution or possibility.

- **Learning** – Think about this in terms of: "We've never done this before; therefore, no single one of us could have the whole answer." Maybe you're creating a new policy or process. Maybe you're developing a new product or service, or expanding into a new geography or industry sector. Whatever the case, hearing from everyone will pay dividends in helping you see the big picture and understand the broader implications of your solution or decision.

- **Gaining Commitment** – There are three things that support this situation:

  ○ You need their psychological buy-in.

  ○ You need them to make it work.

  ○ You want them to have some skin in the game. Anyone who has led a team or been a team member knows that if you get to contribute to the solution, you are much more committed to seeing it through to completion. *Collaborating* gives me that chance to contribute.

There is a nuance or distinction I would like to make. Sometimes, you will choose the *collaborate* tool to determine "what" it is you want to accomplish. And sometimes the "what" has already been decided and you are collaborating about "how" to best achieve the "what." It's critical that you be clear and that everyone who is contributing is clear on whether it is a "what" or "how" solution you're trying to develop. For example, your organization has described a strategy of 20 percent growth over three years. This is the "what." There are many different ways to get to that 20 percent. You can acquire other companies, introduce new products or services, or expand into new geographies. This is the "how." I further suggest that you determine the "what" before you even begin to think about the "how." You have to know what you're trying to achieve.

COLLABORATING SKILLS

The skills required to be a good collaborator are important. If you don't use these skills, your collaboration can break down quickly.

- **Ability to Listen** – We know that some people are good listeners and some are not. I want to share what I call a three-level listening model (another tool in your tool kit).

  ○ **Level 1:** Listening with your ears. This means I can repeat back to you what you just said. It is the lowest level of listening. It doesn't sound too complicated, and we know there are people in meetings who are not listening even at this fundamental level. They are on their phones, emailing, multitasking, not paying attention, or thinking about what they want to say. Don't be that person. Be present and engaged. At a minimum, be able to repeat what another person has said.

  ○ **Level 2:** Listening with your head. If you have accomplished Level 1 listening, you now want to process and analyze what you've heard. How does it connect to what your experience or research tells you? Is it relevant? Can you build on it? Would it work? Does it expand your thinking?

  ○ **Level 3:** Listening with your heart. For many, this sounds too soft or not fact based. In reality, we make many heart choices every day. Then we retrofit the data or facts to justify our

choices. One of my favorite examples relates to hiring inter-
views. I have read about many examples and research around
this scenario. Looking back on my own hiring experiences, I
must admit it is a familiar story:

*Let's say you are scheduled for a one-hour interview and,
at the end of the hour, you will or will not extend an offer
of employment. You have reviewed the candidate's resume
and have your questions ready. The literature tells us that
a majority of us will make up our minds to extend or not
extend an offer at around the fifteen-minute mark. Then
for the remaining forty-five minutes, you hear the candidate's responses through the lens or filter based on our
decision at the fifteen-minute mark. In other words, if you
have chosen to extend an offer, you will interpret the candidate's subsequent responses favorably or vice versa.*

*Now let's review this. How much factual informa-
tion have you gathered in fifteen minutes? Yes, you have
reviewed the resume, and anyone who has done much
hiring knows that resumes tend to be of lesser consideration
in making a formal decision. Further, let's review what
happens in that first fifteen minutes. The candidate walks
in and shakes hands. Here are all the more subtle cues you're
processing. Was it an appropriately firm handshake? Did
the candidate walk in with a confident gait? Did the candidate look you in the eye? Did the candidate smile? Was
the candidate warm? Did you feel a connection?*

*You spend the first several minutes introducing your-
self, describing the role and perhaps the company. After a
self-introduction by the candidate, you start asking your
questions. Based on your subconscious or even unconscious
reaction in the first fifteen minutes, you hear and interpret
the candidate's remaining responses accordingly.*

You may have described this as gut instinct, intuition, or even chemistry. That's what I mean by listening with our hearts. If you are conscious and are on high alert, you'll notice this is happening several times a day. How do you assess colleagues, clients, other drivers on the road, grocery store clerks, conference speakers, and television characters? You may have also heard the old saying: "I'll believe it when I see it." In fact, our brain works the opposite way. "If I believe it, I will see it." If I believe you're smart, I will trust you when you talk. If I believe you aren't smart, I will question, challenge, or ignore what you have to say. This is the essence of our unconscious bias. We are making up stories about others without adequate information. Stereotypes are an outcome of this way of thinking.

And one further bit of research: We often draw conclusions about another person with a blink of an eye, or 250 milliseconds. That's why first impressions are so critical and real. That confident gait, firm handshake, warm smile, and even how you're dressed all create that first impression. Knowing this can help us make better choices. And it all starts with listening.

When *collaborating*, a great many words, facts, data, research, and anecdotal experiences are shared. If you are going to give weight and consideration to what others are saying, be aware of these levels of listening. And this next skill will help you to process it all.

- **Nonthreatening Confrontation** – Various studies have been done that describe behaviors that are most valuable or influential in meetings. One of the most effective is balancing advocacy and inquiry. For example, here is my point of view, my research, my experience—advocating my position. And the other half is inquiring. By allowing another person to also assert their thoughts, we can now integrate solutions or merge perspectives. If listening on all three levels, you will also want to probe and clarify.

   I encourage you to ask questions that start with "how" or "what." For example, "How would that work?" "What additional resources would we need in order to successfully do that?" These questions will keep people engaged and are asked for purposes of learning. Avoid asking questions that start with "why." These questions will often put people on the defensive and can create more conflict. It's as if you are drawing a line in the sand and if you are on one side or the other, you are on the right or wrong side of the line.

The second most influential or effective participants in meetings are those who inquire more than they advocate. And the least effective are those who advocate, advocate, advocate. I can imagine that a face or name may have just popped into your head. We can all recall those people or those experiences. No matter what another person says, this person keeps coming back to his or her idea. Pretty soon, you just tune them out. You check your phone, take a personal break, or start thinking about something unrelated. They pretend to be *collaborating* when they are really *competing*. And that's why it is so important to be clear about a gathering being a collaborative effort and defining what you mean by *collaborating*.

- **Analyzing Input/Identifying Concerns** – As with any brainstorming session, a lot of ideas and information are shared. I encourage you to identify—ahead of a meeting—your decision criteria, and make sure you share it with the group. Decision criteria might include cost, available resources, timelines, competitive advantage, regulatory requirements, contract terms and conditions, legal requirements, or reflections of yours or your organization's values, principles, or brand. As ideas and information are shared and the time for decision-making arrives, you will have to assess the best aspects of the information shared. You may also discover that you haven't explored all of the items on your decision criteria list. If that's the case, you'll want to ensure appropriate time, focus, and consideration be allocated to those remaining topics. This will ensure a more comprehensive decision with fewer problems as the decision is executed. A little extra time on the front end will pay big dividends on the back end, resulting in less "re-work," less tension, greater productivity, and a better chance at delivering a successful solution.

- **Facilitating** – Collaboration is a mindset and a process. From the process perspective, you want to ensure that you hear from everyone. I often use a process called check-in and checkout. These are tools in your tool kit. The value of having everyone speak at the beginning of a significant gathering (check-in) is that once their voice is in the room, they are more likely to speak up in the following discussion. We often call these practices "ice breakers." They are an important component, especially in collaborative settings.

    Check-in questions might be: "What do you hope to accomplish in this meeting?" or "How can you best contribute to our objective today?" (Notice that the questions start with "what" and "how.") The responses to these questions will help the facilitator know when to invite people to contribute in specific and useful ways.

    The role of the facilitator is specific and includes **the following**:

    ○ Creates the agenda with the meeting leader. This includes meeting objectives, who should be invited, timeline, and decision criteria.

    ○ Manages activities during the meeting, ensuring adequate time for every topic on the agenda, recording decisions, questions, and follow-up items.

    ○ Ensures participants are engaged and involved and that each participant has an opportunity to contribute their ideas as well as probe and clarify others' ideas.

○ Recaps the important points of the meeting to ensure alignment as people leave the meeting. This includes agreed-upon items and who has responsibility for those items, and next steps as appropriate.

It is also useful to note that it is difficult to be both a facilitator and a participant. If your gathering is to resolve or decide a big issue (new, high-risk, high-visibility, big stakes), bring in someone to facilitate so that you can fully participate without having to also manage the process. When you try to do both roles, it is often confusing to other participants. They are wondering if you're speaking as a facilitator or a content contributor. This doesn't mean you have to hire a facilitator, though that may be a viable option. Choose someone who understands the facilitator role and can be detached from the outcome.

Coming full circle from check-in, checkout questions are a great "pulse-checking" tool. They give everyone a chance—in the moment—to describe how they feel about the meeting. Their comments might reflect thoughts about content shared, the facilitation process, and decisions made. It will also help you know if there are some follow-on conversations needed. Check-out questions could be: "What stands out for you regarding where we are as we leave this meeting?" "How will you share the direction of this project based on today's meeting?" (Notice again the "what" and "how" questions.)

These checkout questions also prompt people to stop and think versus moving on to the next meeting. They attach additional meaning to the process and the outcomes of a collaborative meeting. Inevitably, these questions also help participants craft their narrative on how they will talk about the particular solution or decision.

OVERUSE OF COLLABORATING

Even though many of us see the valuable benefits of *collaborating*, this tool can be overused. This is my story for sure. As an extrovert and lifelong learner, I love talking to and hearing from others on almost any topic.

- **Too Much Time on Trivial Matters/Work Overload** – Not every decision or solution requires collaboration. As you know, you can spend endless hours in meetings that consume your days. You may even find that at the end of the day, you have not marked off one thing on your to-do list. If that's the case, you either work longer hours at the office, bring your work home, or even find yourself missing deadlines. Work hard to be thoughtful and intentional when it comes to using the collaborative approach in the situations noted earlier.

- **Diffused Responsibility** – Some people fear that if a solution or decision was developed as a team, then no *one* person is going to be responsible. I was working with a COO once who actually said, "If this project goes south, I want one throat to choke." I shuddered at his comment for so many reasons. The important thing here is that you are clear about assigning roles and responsibilities just as you would on any group assignment, and hold people accountable accordingly.

- **Others May Take Advantage** – Another way of thinking about this is: "Beware the *competer* in *collaborator's* clothing." When you invite people to a meeting and tell them it is a collaborative meeting, hold true to your process. We have all experienced the person in a meeting who has the right answer and he or she won't move off their position. Even as different people bring their respective ideas and experiences, this person keeps repeating their same point again and again. Clearly, they aren't there to collaborate.

The role of the facilitator is important in this situation. When I have been in the role of facilitator, I have gently pushed back and asked the person if they are open to hearing others' views or expanding their own. I have also asked the person to leave a meeting (privately while on break) if they are disrupting the meeting or preventing it from getting to a true collaborative solution. It hasn't happened often, and I do so very respectfully, acknowledging that they may be ready to come to a decision, but that as a group we aren't there yet. As you can imagine, this is most tricky when the offender has the most authority or positional power in the room. I then circle back, and we discuss whether they truly want a collaborative process or if they are going through the motions simply to declare they gave everyone the opportunity to speak up. This is often described as the sham of collaboration.

The key message here is not to let someone derail your collaborative process. This is why the clarity of your communication, declaring it a collaborative process on the front-end, is so important.

UNDERUSE OF COLLABORATING

Collaborating can be underused just as it can be overused. Here are some examples.

- **Loss of Mutual Gains** – If you don't give everyone who will be involved in making a decision an opportunity to contribute their best thinking, you often end up with an incomplete or suboptimized result. You may not understand the ripple effects of your decision or solution. This results in surprises, last-minute fire drills, unhappy customers, lost credibility, and "re-work."

- **Low Empowerment/Lack of Commitment** – If you are the person always telling instead of inviting others' input, people tend to wait for your directives rather than offer their own thoughts or ideas. Over time they become order takers rather than critical thinkers with a leadership mindset. I often say that the chronic order givers will get malicious compliance rather than empowered engagement. To truly gain commitment you need to engage their heads, hearts, and hands in determining a solution or making a decision.

- **Loss of Innovation** – During the collaborative process is when generative thinking occurs, building on one another's ideas and creating solutions no one person could have come up with on their own. Underuse of collaboration potentially results in the loss of new, creative, innovative solutions or decisions. Having diversity of thought, experience, functional expertise, and life perspective is beyond valuable in creating new possibilities, delivering results, and enriching relationships.

REFLECTION:

Think of a time when you have collaborated in a conflict.

How was collaborating an effective or ineffective strategy?

Do you have a situation where you are currently collaborating in a conflict?

Is that a strategic choice or a default response?

COMPROMISING

The *compromising* approach falls into the middle of the framework when both results and relationships are of medium or mid-importance. I also see this approach as another way of describing a negotiating approach. You will feel strongly about some issues, and others will be negotiable. There is give and take on both sides, thus the tagline: "Let's make a deal." An important part of this is feeling that you got as much as you gave—that feeling of reciprocity and fairness.

	Tagline	"Let's make a deal"
Compromising	**Situation**	• Reaching resolution with equal power • Creating temporary solutions • Dealing with time constraints
	Skills	• Negotiating • Finding middle ground • Making concessions • Assessing value to a situation or "line item"
	Overuse	• Lose sight of the big picture/Long-term goals • Lack of trust/Cynical climate
	Underuse	• Unable to negotiate effectively • Unnecessary confrontations/Frequent power struggles

COMPROMISING SITUATIONS

If you determine compromise as the most effective strategy, you clearly acknowledge that the two parties are entering the conversation or interaction with the willingness to engage in a give-and-take exchange. The following are considerations for when *compromising* will best fit the situation.

- **Reaching Resolution with Equal Power** – Each party is coming to the table with equal authority and power, regardless of positional power—*and* it is important to ensure alignment on this equality before you get started. This can be a tricky situation. Make sure you know what authority you have, as well as what you can give up and what your priorities are for your asks. If you need to include your boss or some other subject-matter expert, make sure you do adequate planning and preparation before moving into the conversation. If you are extending authority to someone who works for you, make sure you provide them your thoughts, expectations, and boundaries. And as conversations progress, continue to provide support to your team member, helping them build strong negotiating skills.

- **Creating Temporary Solutions** – *Compromising* can be a short-term as well as a long-term solution. You may be able to agree on some imminent issues that have a deadline or are critical-path items before you can move ahead to achieve your long-term objectives. My caution is to make sure that short-term decisions or solutions don't limit you or come back to haunt you in the long run. Start with the end in mind. Take as comprehensive a view as you can, knowing that new information will surface and you have to be ready to flex accordingly.

- **Dealing with Time Constraints** – If the conversation to resolve a conflict or reach a decision is based on a longer term project, you may want to break it down into phases, stages, or milestones. No matter what you're working on, you need to be able to communicate progress and report on status. Breaking a big project, task, decision, or resolution into smaller parts is often helpful in reaching an agreement. Otherwise, it can seem so big or overwhelming that you can become paralyzed, which serves no one.

COMPROMISING SKILLS

Compromising skills align with negotiating skills. I will not attempt to teach you in-depth negotiating skills; I will give you a macro or high-level view of negotiating.

- **Negotiating** – Get a blank sheet of paper and draw a horizontal line across the middle of it. Note those concerns that are not negotiable below the line. These are the elements you either declare are givens, off the table, or ones you will *compete* for. Above the line, note those concerns you are willing to give up. I'll discuss that further in the following paragraphs. And last, make a list of things you want. You are now ready to begin the *compromising* or *negotiating* process.

- **Finding Middle Ground** – The skill needed to know what goes above and below that horizontal line reflects our ability to find middle ground. Keep in mind that both the result you want to achieve and the relationship you want to nurture are key criteria in making this decision. There are no firm guidelines. Consider as many variables as possible—time, money, people, customer impact—and ensure alignment with key stakeholders in your scope of responsibility. Play out scenarios to better understand the ripple effects of your position.

- **Making Concessions** – By its very definition, *compromising* requires you to be willing to make concessions. In my experience, there are two tones that making concessions can take. The first involves one person convincing another that they should be forever grateful and that giving up whatever that person is giving up is a big deal. The second is more of a "we're in this together and I want to be fair and reasonable" tone. The first prioritizes the results I want; the second also considers the relationship. Be thoughtful and intentional in tone and language as well as determining where the line goes and what is above and below it.

- **Assessing Value to a Situation or "Line Item"** – When you list your above-the-line items, you want to place them in priority order. What is the first thing you are willing to give up in exchange for something you want? What is the second? And so on. In addition, if possible, assign a monetary value to each line item. This ensures that you are getting equivalent value for each item you give up. In simple terms, if your number-one concern to give up is worth $100 and the person with whom you're interacting has a number-one item to exchange with you and it is worth $50, you will want to ask what their number-two item is to ensure greater equivalency of your $100 item. As we all know, not everything can be assigned a direct and specific value.

  An example of this would be a request for an accelerated project deadline. Your *compromising* position or offer might be to ask for additional resources in order to accelerate the deadline. It could require reallocating staff from another project to yours or approving a budget increase to hire contractors. My caution on this particular scenario is to make sure that adding resources will truly enable you to deliver on an accelerated date. I always think of the analogy someone told me early in my career—"nine women being pregnant for one month each cannot give birth to a baby." In other words, throwing resources at a project doesn't always solve the problem.

OVERUSE OF COMPROMISING

If you are always trying to "make a deal" or please everyone else by giving in or giving up, you can get yourself in trouble.

- **Lose Sight of the Big Picture/Long-Term Goals** – I always think of the line: "I'll give you one of these for two of those."

It's basically a "this-for-that" exchange. If you focus too much on the line item exchanges, you can suboptimize the long-term goals, objectives, or benefits you're trying to achieve. Think about it this way—you need a microscope on one eye and a telescope on the other eye, seeing the detail and balancing it with the big-picture objectives. Doing this effectively requires you to plan effectively and understand the ripple effects of your decision.

- **Lack of Trust/Cynical Climate** – This is a "watch out" when certain behaviors are repeated over time. Let's go back to that horizontal line in the middle of the page. What you include above and below the line is significantly important. If you tell your team that what is below the line is uncompromisable, and then you move the line, resulting in something now becoming compromisable, you can lose the trust and confidence of your team to stand up for what you previously stated.

  Let's be clear, sometimes such decisions you make are overridden or superseded by your leadership, your clients, or market conditions. The emphasis here is on a pattern of such behavior (moving the line) that generates the mistrust and may even elicit cynicism when you declare where the line is. Another important leadership choice is not to make promises you can't keep or that are tentative at best. Work hard to get alignment before you make such promises.

UNDERUSE OF COMPROMISING

Ah, the give and take of life. We all know you can't get everything you want all the time. And we also know you rarely get all or nothing. As you work through conflicts or decisions, you want to always consider the *compromising* option. At the same time, it doesn't mean you push hard to get everything without being willing to *compromise*. That looks too much like overuse of *competing*.

- **Unable to Negotiate Effectively** – Every leader needs to be able to negotiate effectively with their teams, peers, bosses, customers, vendors, and various potential stakeholders. The clarity and intentionality of planning a conversation or presenting a position or recommendation requires strong analytical and strategic skills. Where do you draw the line? What is above and below the line? How do you prioritize and assess value to what you are willing to compromise? How do you prioritize and assess the value of what your colleague is offering? This is just the starting point. It is worth your while to take a negotiating class and become proficient in the art of negotiating.

- **Unnecessary Confrontations/Frequent Power Struggles** – We all know *that* person—the one you dread because meeting or working with them is always a struggle. They rarely consider another's point of view or perspective. To the extreme they can also be viewed as a bully. They seem to enjoy a good fight just for the sake of a fight. In short, don't be that person. It is not reflective of a true leader's brand.

I would be remiss if I didn't add that many women are experienced negotiators. You learn by being a mom. Do any of these examples sound familiar? "Eat your vegetables and you can have dessert." "Clean up your room and you can go to your friend's house." "Make good grades and you can have . . . [*fill in the blank*]." The trick is for you to recognize you may be a better negotiator than you think you are and to apply this same skill in your professional life.

REFLECTION:

Think of a time when you have compromised in a conflict.

How was compromising an effective or ineffective strategy?

Do you have a situation where you are currently compromising in a conflict?

Is that a strategic choice or a default response?

You now have a considerable amount of information regarding the five Response Modes or tools in your tool kit. Now let's look at some additional tools that can help you apply these strategies effectively.

CONFLICT STRATEGY PREPARATION CHECKLIST

The next step is to determine and refine our thinking around what tool to use in a given situation.

The first question is: **"Which is more important, the relationship or the result?"** If the relationship is of high importance, you will consider accommodating or collaborating. If the result is of high importance, you will consider competing or collaborating (see framework on page 248). I recommend you use a simple approach to answering this question: low, medium, or high. If multiple people are involved, the answer to this question could potentially be different for each one. Take your time. Be clear. Be thoughtful and intentional.

The second question is: **"Who is the conflict with?"** This seems like a straightforward question, and yet, the answer can take many forms.

One possibility is that you and a colleague are engaged in a conflict or are trying to make a decision. You find out that your colleague is merely doing what their boss tells them to do. Is your conflict with your colleague or your colleague's boss? Are you also doing the bidding of your boss? It is important that the people who are attached to a specific outcome be actively engaged in the conversations. The back-and-forth of these "surrogate" conversations can create considerable churn and result in contentious relationships. That said, we have all had experience in carrying out tasks as delegated by our bosses. The "watch out" is that you end up being the "fall girl" for your boss. In other words, you have all the hard conversations and get the predictable reputation associated with that.

Another possibility is that we declare we have a conflict with a certain department, business unit, customer, company, or even a geographic region. It sounds a little silly *and* you can't have a conversation with a department, business unit, or region to resolve a conflict. You have to have a conversation with a human being. Determining who holds the contrary or opposing view is critical in efficiently and effectively having a productive conversation. I was teaching a leadership class for a client on this topic and rhetorically asked, "Who is the conflict with?" It was an intact team, and almost in unison they answered, "Europe." When I started laughing, they asked me why I thought that was funny. I told them it is pretty hard to have a conversation with a continent, especially one that speaks several languages. Needless to say, clarity on who the conversation is with is crucial.

The third question is: **"Is this a 'what' or 'how' conflict?"** It is important to be clear and aligned on *what* you are trying to accomplish first. If you don't get agreement on that, you certainly can't determine *how* to get there. I'm reminded of a line in *Alice in Wonderland*: "If you don't know where you are going, any road will get you there." You must know where you are going. Clues to determine whether you're aligned are conversations that go round and round, lots of tangential stories or distractions, or trying to find solutions for problems that don't have direct or immediate relevance to the conflict you're trying to solve.

The last question is: **"Which of the five conflict mode situations most resembles my situation?"** For example, are you trying to reduce tension or buy time (avoiding)? Are you trying to create goodwill (accommodating)? Are you standing up for vital issues such as values, ethics, fairness (competing)? Are you trying to gain the psychological buy-in and commitment of another person or team of people (collaborating)? Are you ready to do some give-and-take to resolve the conflict (compromising)?

By getting really clear on the preceding questions, you are now ready to display your skills and craft your strategy, key messages, and determine the best language to arrive at the best solution.

BE PREPARED

I also want to share an important concept when considering conflict conversations: *Just because you are invited into a conflict does not mean you have to accept the invitation.* If you are expecting a conflict, you can prepare by using the conflict strategy checklist previously described. Let's talk about when you're not expecting to enter into a potential conflict conversation and are not prepared to strategically address the issues.

Imagine that you are going to a weekly staff meeting and you think it will be a run-of-the-mill, passive meeting. You're prepared to share your project status and to listen to others' updates. Unexpectedly, one of your colleagues declares a problem that you or someone on your team is causing. You are caught off guard because you know nothing about it and aren't prepared. This is the moment of choice! Don't engage in a conversation that you're not prepared to have. In other words, don't accept the invitation. Here is the language I would use in that moment:

> "This sounds like an important topic to you. I didn't come to this meeting prepared to discuss it, and I wouldn't want to give you an incomplete or ineffective response. Can we meet right after this meeting so that I can understand the situation and your specific concerns?"

Regardless of your colleague's response, stay true to not getting pulled into a conversation you're not prepared to have. This language is professional and respectful. It lets your colleague know you realize the issue is important to him or her and you don't want to be cavalier or casual in addressing it. You also don't want to make commitments without talking to your team members and hearing their perspectives on the situation. I know when I've engaged in these kinds of conversations and made incomplete or ill-advised commitments, I've almost always regretted it. My team has wanted to kill me for not getting their input, and they certainly didn't feel I supported them. It has also often caused retractions or "re-work" when all sides of the story are shared and understood. This can create even more stress and tension between you and your colleague or your teams.

Do make sure you follow through on your commitment to talk with your team and then come back to your colleague to have the conversation. This is an example of a short-term or temporary avoid strategy. Once you have all the facts, you can then go to your strategy checklist, having thoughtfully and intentionally determined which conflict response tool you want to use. And one last thought, by taking this approach, you are not giving your power away by allowing someone else to draw you into a potential conflict conversation you are not ready to have. Stand strong.

THE LANGUAGE OF CONFLICT

I strongly encourage you to use the language and concepts offered here. For instance, if you choose to accommodate someone, you can say, "You want red, and I want blue. Our relationship is important to me. I am happy to accommodate your red approach and will support it fully." You have just resolved a conflict in three sentences.

A second scenario is that your colleague wants a certain something. You may have a different want, though you are willing to be flexible on certain aspects. You might say, "I can support these details you want, and there are a few others I too feel strongly about. Let's see if we can agree on some give-and-take items and reach a compromise to our mutual satisfaction." This example lays the groundwork for additional steps with a clear strategy of negotiation.

The previous two examples would be considered to be the easier ones. The example you often dread the most is one in which you both are in *compete* mode—the result is most important to you both, and you are in clear disagreement. This is a situation in which I recommend the **three-column tool**. Take a piece of paper (or a white board or three pieces of paper). The heading for column 1 is "Things We Agree On." In this column, write down all the things on which you can agree. This might include budget, timeline, deliverables, available staff, pertinent contract terms and conditions, regulatory requirements, and so on. Write down as many things as you can. Once you agree on what is included in this column, these things are no longer in play relative to your conflict.

Things We Agree On	Willing to Compromise	What's Left

Now you can move on to column 2. The heading for this column is "Willing to Compromise." Here you determine, agree upon, and write down those things that you and the other person are willing to engage in a give-and-take exchange. This column might include a conversation on moving a deadline to an earlier date if the other person is willing to reallocate resources to work on the deadline deliverables. Once you have agreed on the give-and-take exchange, you can now move those items into column 1, "Things We Agree On."

And finally, we move to column 3: "What's Left." Having used this approach for over twenty years, I can tell you that about half the time there is nothing left to put in column 3. What you have done is break down what was a big potential conflict situation into smaller pieces, and you've resolved those smaller items one at a time.

The other half of the time there is generally a short list of outstanding items to resolve. You now have a couple of choices: 1) You can escalate these remaining issues—more on that in a moment, or 2) You can take each outstanding item through the three-column approach. For some, this may seem a bit tedious. You may want to take a break and come back to these items at a later time. Of course, there are many variables to consider. Are the outstanding items considered to be critical path items and, therefore, ones that have to be resolved before you can move things forward? If so, your break may be a short one, perhaps only a few hours or day or two. If resolving the outstanding items doesn't require immediate resolution, your break can be a longer one. During that break you may want to do some additional research to inform your perspective and, therefore, your approach for when you come back together.

Now, let's talk about escalating the outstanding items. Again, you have some choices. I encourage you to be clear about your position as well as the other person's position. You need to support your position with facts and have the courage of your convictions to present your position. I also encourage you to escalate *out* before you escalate *up*. Is there a subject matter expert you can call upon to help resolve the issue? Are there best practices that might help? Do you have a strong business case on which to reinforce your position? I would want to explore every avenue before having to escalate up to our bosses. You don't want your boss to think you can't resolve your own conflicts or challenges. Share this thinking with your colleague. It may give both of you renewed energy to resolve the outstanding items. Only as a last resort do you take it to your boss to resolve.

If you find it necessary to escalate to your boss, here are some additional considerations. Make sure you let your boss know you have resolved all other items and that you only need him or her to weigh in on these few items. Be specific with what you need. The last thing you want to do is open up all the items you have already resolved. In other words, no second-guessing. Narrow the scope. You and your colleague will want to align your strategies on escalating to your bosses. Your goal is to strive for good outcomes. Stay focused on the outcomes. Agree on deadlines for a decision or resolution.

A few last points as we wrap up this topic of conflict management. If at all possible, have these conversations face-to-face. I know that this is not always possible. Use a virtual platform that includes video as an alternative. Phone is your next best option. Never try to resolve conflicts using email, texts, or some sort of group app. You don't get the benefit of body language, tone, or volume. If an email has gone back and forth without resolving the issue, schedule a meeting or a phone call.

Last, minimize resolving conflicts in public. When you have an audience, the conversation often becomes fodder for the rumor mill and may lead to damaging gossip. Only include those people directly involved in resolving the conflict, and keep the discussion private. Two women having a conflict is often seen as more newsworthy. Remember that stereotype that all women must get along all of the time. This is not a realistic expectation. Women aren't always going to agree. And when we do disagree, we want to proceed with a leadership mindset. We are civil and professional about it. We don't take everything personally, and we generally maintain a strong relationship post-disagreement. Don't be the person who starts or spreads the gossip. Be the person who models behaviors that change the stereotype that if women can't agree, there must be something wrong with them.

Here are some questions for reflection on this topic. Don't be afraid of conflict. You can do this!

REFLECTION:

Describe your comfort level with conflict.

What gives you the courage and clarity to engage in potential conflict conversations?

What prevents you from engaging in potential conflict conversations?

Which conflict response mode is your default pattern?

How will you build your skills and awareness to feel more comfortable and confident in using all five Conflict Response Modes?

What immediate or near-term opportunity do you have that would allow you to apply what you've learned about managing conflict?

PART 2 DISCUSSION QUESTIONS

I encourage you to answer the questions individually before discussing them as a group. You want to do your own personal work. Once you hear others' responses, you can add, change, or even delete items in your own responses. Remember, women learn through stories. Share yours freely and deeply, and listen as others do the same.

SECTION REFLECTION QUESTIONS:

What did you learn about yourself while reading this section?

What stands out for you about women supporting women?

What stands out for you about building and sustaining trust?

continued

What stands out for you about setting and maintaining boundaries?

What stands out for you about trusting your intuition?

What stands out for you about managing conflict?

What are three things you'll do differently going forward based on what you've learned?

EPILOGUE

I close this book with a poem that I read at the end of all my long-term programs.

"Embrace Your Own Greatness"

Live your life through your own eyes
Hold close your grandest vision
Of yourself
Do not compromise your greatness
For another's vision
Talk your own language
Express your own soul
You owe nothing to another
Only to yourself
Be honest with yourself and your desires
Speak of your highest thoughts
Be all you held in your childhood dreams
No one can take away your power
Unless you are the one to give it away
Walk with your head held high
So you can see everything clearly
Decide daily who you wish to be
Create your own moments with wisdom
Carve out your future with clarity

Become your desires
Expand your horizons
Leave yesterdays behind
Run toward tomorrow
Change your mind often
Learn how to flow with the river
Close your eyes and let life take you
Go where your heart leads
Never give up
Don't believe that mistakes
Are destroyers of life
See them as gifts for future success
Dance on rainbows
Meet fairies
Sing with angels
And always give thanks
For the treasure that is life

—Lynette Ann Lane

As you've worked through the activities, answered or journaled about the reflections questions, and pondered your own examples, I hope you have discovered or rediscovered more of the greatness within you. Whether you've done this individually or as some sort of group activity, I hope your journey was a rich one with delightful insights along the way.

As I write these closing words, I have an image of you wrapping your arms around yourself—embracing your powerful self. My wish in everything I do is to add value—to my family, my friends, my team, my clients, and my community. I hope my wish has come true in service to YOU! And here's to women supporting women!

APPENDIX

LIST OF TOOLS

INTRODUCTION:

- Foundational Elements Concepts

CHAPTER 1:

- Powerful Women Are . . .
- Positional, Relational, and Personal Power
- Power Sources

CHAPTER 2:

- Stereotypes—Masculine and Feminine Attributes
- Invisible Differences
- The Female and Male Brains
- Impostor Cycle

CHAPTER 3:

- Values Checklist—Personal and Professional
- Risk Assessment
- StrengthsFinder
- Anatomy of a Compelling Vision
- Creator vs. Reactor

CHAPTER 4:

- Misogyny Questions
- My Support System Table

CHAPTER 5:

- Reina Trust and Betrayal Model®
- Expectations Menu
- Reina Betrayal Continuum®
- 7-Step Feedback Model
- Ladder of Inference
- Feeling Words *(See Additional Tools.)*
- Reina Seven Steps for Healing®

CHAPTER 6:

- "Big Rocks" Priority Setting
- 7 Ports of Life—Managing our Time with Intentionality
- Delegate-Check-Review Triangle
- Checks and Balances Template
- Setting Boundaries Principles

CHAPTER 7:

- Six Distinct Ways Intuition Communicates

CHAPTER 8:

- Group Trust Model

CHAPTER 9:

- Conflict Response Modes
- Conflict Strategy Preparation Checklist
- 3-Column Approach for Working Through Conflict
- 3-Level Listening Model
- Check-in/Check-out

RECOMMENDED READING & RESOURCES

FEMALE RELATIONSHIPS

1. Brown, Brené. *Dare to Lead: Brave Work. Tough Conversations. Whole Hearts.* New York: Random House, 2018.

2. Cuddy, Amy. *Presence: Bringing Your Boldest Self to Your Biggest Challenges.* New York: Little, Brown & Company, 2015.

3. Doyle, Anne. *Powering Up: How America's Women Achievers Become Leaders.* Bloomington, IN: Xlibris, Corp., 2011.

4. Evans, Gail. *She Wins, You Win.* New York: Gotham Books, 2003.

5. Gates, Melinda. *The Moment of Lift: How Empowering Women Changes the World.* New York: Flatiron Books, 2019.

6. Ginsburg, Ruth Bader, Mary Hartnett, and Wendy Williams. *My Own Words.* New York: Simon & Schuster, 2016.

7. Halter, Jeffery Tobias. *Why Women: The Leadership Imperative to Advancing Women & Engaging Men.* Marietta, GA: Fushian LLC, 2015.

8. Helgesen, Sally, and Marshall Goldsmith. *How Women Rise: Break the 12 Habits Holding You Back from Your Next Raise, Promotion or Job.* New York: Hachette Books, 2018.

9. Helgesen, Sally, and Julie Johnson. *The Female Vision: Women's Real Power at Work.* Oakland, CA: Berrett-Koehler Publishers, Inc., 2010.

10. Krawcheck, Sallie. *Own It: The Power of Women at Work.* New York: Crown Business, 2017.

11.　Lesser, Elizabeth. *Cassandra Speaks: When Women Are the Storytellers, the Human Story Changes.* Harper Wave, 2020.

12.　Litwin, Anne. *New Rules for Women: Revolutionizing the Way Women Work Together.* Arnold, MD: Third Bridge Press, 2014.

13.　Michaelis, David. *Eleanor.* New York: Simon & Schuster, 2020.

14.　Obama, Michelle. *Becoming.* New York: Crown Publishing, 2018.

15.　Perez, Caroline Criado. *Invisible Women: Data Bias in a World Designed for Men.* New York: Harry N. Abrams, 2019.

16.　Sandberg, Sheryl. *Lean In: Women, Work, and the Will to Lead.* New York: Alfred A. Knopf, 2013.

17.　Tannen, Deborah. *You Just Don't Understand: Women and Men in Conversation.* New York: William Morrow Paperbacks, 2007.

18.　Yousafzai, Malala. *I am Malala: The Girl Who Stood Up for Education and Was Shot by the Taliban.* New York: Little, Brown & Co., 2013.

MALE AND FEMALE BRAIN

1.　Amen, Daniel G. *Change Your Brain, Change Your Life.* New York: Harmony, 2015.

2.　Barron-Cohen, Simon. *The Essential Difference: The Truth about the Male & Female Brain.* New York: Basic Books, 2003.

3.　Brizendine, Louann. *The Female Brain.* New York: Three Rivers Press, 2006.

4.　Brizendine, Louann. *The Male Brain.* New York: Three Rivers Press, 2010.

5.　Doidge, Norman. *The Brain That Changes Itself: Stories of Personal Triumph from the Frontiers of Brain Science.* New York: Penguin Books, 2007.

6.　Eagleman, David. *Incognito: The Secret Lives of the Brain.* New York: Vintage Books, 2011.

7.　Pinker, Steven. *How the Mind Works.* New York: W. W. Norton & Co., 1998.

8.　Pradeep, A. K. *The Buying Brain: Secrets for Selling to the Subconscious Mind.* Hoboken, NJ: John Wiley & Sons, Inc., 2010.

IMPOSTOR PHENOMENON

1. Clance, Pauline Rose, PhD. *The Impostor Phenomenon—Overcoming the Fear that Haunts Your Success.* Atlanta, GA: Peachtree Publishers LTD., 1985.

2. Kay, Katty, and Claire Shipman. *The Confidence Code.* New York: Harper Business, 2014.

MINDFULNESS AND MEDITATION

1. Bennett, Bija. *Breathing into Life: Recovering Wholeness through Mind, Body & Breath.* Center City, MN: Hazelden Books, 1993.

2. De Mello, Anthony. *Awareness: The Perils and Opportunities of Reality.* New York: Image, 1992.

3. Kornfield, Jack, Ph.D. *Meditation for Beginners.* Louisville, CO: Sounds True, 2008.

4. Myss, Carolyn, PhD. *Anatomy of the Spirit: The 7 Stages of Power & Healing.* New York: Random House, 1996.

TRUST

1. Bracey, Hyler, PhD. *Building Trust: How to Get It! How to Keep It!* Scotts Valley, CA: CreateSpace Independent Publishing Platform, 2002.

2. Covey, Stephen M. R. *The Speed of Trust.* New York: Simon & Schuster, 2006.

3. Dreamer, Oriah Mountain. *The Invitation.* New York: Harper Collins Publishers, 1999.

4. Feltman, Charles. *The Thin Book of Trust: An Essential Primer for Building Trust at Work.* Bend, OR: Thin Book Publishing, 2009.

5. Andrea Mayfield and Christina Williams, Ph.D. *Trust Talk™ (Dialogue Cards).* Bend, OR: Thin Book Publishing, 2006.

6. Lencioni, Patrick. *The Five Dysfunctions of a Team: A Leadership Fable.* Hoboken, NJ: Jossey-Bass, 2002.

7. Reina, Dennis & Michelle, PhDs. *Trust and Betrayal in the Workplace, 3rd Edition.* Berrett-Koehler Publishers, Inc., 2015.

8. Reina, Dennis & Michelle, PhDs. *Rebuilding Trust in the Workplace*, Berrett-Koehler Publishers, Inc., 2010.

9. Reina Trust Building® Journey Online Platform - Trust Bits® - bite size Trust Building® bits of information, videos, tools, resources, activities and exercise delivered to email weekly

10. Reina Trust Pack® Cards – 54 Trust Building Flash Cards to help you practice and live Trust Behaviors daily

11. Seashore, Charles, Edith Seashore, and Gerald Weinberg. *What Did You Say? The Art of Giving and Receiving Feedback.* Columbia, MD: Bingham House Books, 1997.

12. Van der Kolk, Bessel, M.D. *The Body Keeps the Score: Brain, Mind and Body in the Healing of Trauma.* New York: Viking, 2014.

13. Wall, Cynthia L. *The Courage to Trust: A Guide to Building Deep and Lasting Relationships.* Oakland, CA: New Harbinger Publications, Inc., 2004.

CONFLICT

1. Patterson, Kerry, Joseph Grenny, Ron McMillan, and Al Switzler. *Crucial Conversations: Tools for Talking When Stakes are High.* New York: McGraw-Hill Education, 2011.

2. Scott, Susan. *Fierce Conversations.* New York: Berkley Books, 2004.

DIVERSITY, EQUITY, AND INCLUSION

1. Banagji, Mahzarin R., and Anthony G. Greenwald. *Blindspot: Hidden Biases of Good People.* New York: Delacorte Press, 2013.

2. Bell, Ella, and Stella Nkomo. *Our Separate Ways: Black and White Women and the Struggle for Professional Identity.* Boston: Harvard Business School Press, 2001.

3. Wilkerson, Isabel. *Caste: The Origins of Our Discontents.* New York: Random House, 2020.

ADDITIONAL TOOLS

FEELING WORDS

HAPPY	SAD	ANGRY	DOUBTFUL	MISCELLANEOUS
festive	sorrowful	contemptuous	unbelieving	torn
contented	unhappy	restless	skeptical	mixed-up
relaxed	depressed	irritated	distrustful	envious
calm	melancholy	enraged	suspicious	jealous
complacent	gloomy	furious	dubious	preoccupied
satisfied	somber	annoyed	uncertain	cruel
serene	dismal	inflamed	questioning	distant
comfortable	heavy-hearted	provoked	evasive	bored
peaceful	quiet	offended	wavering	hypocritical
joyous	mournful	sullen	hesitant	phony
ecstatic	dreadful	indignant	perplexed	fake
enthusiastic	dreary	irate	indecisive	two-faced
inspired	flat	wrathful	hopeless	cooperative
glad	blah	cross	defeated	burdened
pleased	dull	sulky	pessimistic	played out
grateful	in the dumps	bitter	confused	hopeful
cheerful	sullen	frustrated		
excited	moody	grumpy	**PHYSICAL**	**AFRAID**
cheery	sulky	boiling	taut	fearful
lighthearted	out of sorts	fuming	uptight	frightened
buoyant	low	stubborn	immobilized	timid
carefree	discontented	belligerent	paralyzed	wishy-washy
surprised	discouraged	confused	tense	shaky
optimistic	disappointed	awkward	stretched	apprehensive
spirited	concerned	bewildered	hollow	fidgety
vivacious	sympathetic		empty	terrified
brisk	compassionate	**FEARLESS**	frisky	panicky
sparkling	choked up	encouraged	strong	tragic
merry	embarrassed	courageous	weak	hysterical
generous	shameful	confident	sweaty	alarmed
hilarious	ashamed	secure	breathless	cautious
exhilarated	useless	independent	nauseated	shocked
jolly	worthless	reassured	sluggish	horrified
playful	ill at ease	bold	weary	insecure
elated	weepy	brave	repulsed	impatient
jubilant	vacant	daring	tired	nervous
thrilled		heroic	alive	dependent
restful	**HURT**	hardy	firm	anxious
silly	injured	determined	hard	pressured
giddy	isolated	loyal	light	worried
	offended	proud		suspicious
EAGER	distressed	impulsive	**AFFECTIONATE**	hesitant
keen	pained		soft	awed
earnest	suffering	**INTERESTED**	close	dismayed
intent	afflicted	concerned	loving	scared
zealous	worried	fascinated	sexy	cowardly
ardent	aching	engrossed	tender	threatened
avid	crushed	absorbed	seductive	appalled
anxious	heartbroken	excited	warm	petrified
proud	cold	curious	open	gutless
excited	upset	inquisitive	appealing	edgy
desirous	lonely	inquiring	aggressive	panicky
	despair	creative	passionate	
	tortured	sincere		
	pathetic			

Feeling Words © by the NTL Institute for Applied Behavioral Science.

CREDITS

ABOUT THE AUTHOR

MARSHA CLARK is an executive coach, training facilitator, and independent consultant who founded her own company in 2000. Marsha's passion is supporting women in their personal and professional development. She has gained international acclaim for her programs that enable women to explore, discover, and optimize their potential. Prior to starting her own business, Marsha was a corporate vice president for Electronic Data Systems. During almost twenty-one years with EDS, she held a variety of roles with ever-increasing responsibility. Marsha has a master of science in organization development from American University in Washington, DC. Marsha's reach is extensive, touching the lives of women across nations and professions. She is sought as a keynote conversationalist and is known as an advocate and supporter of women and girls. Marsha is a widow with one married son and three delightful grandchildren. When she is not teaching or coaching, she enjoys reading and spending time with family and friends.